By the Same Author

Park-Street Papers
John Greenleaf Whittier: A Memoir
Walt Whitman
The Amateur Spirit
A Study of Prose Fiction
The Powers at Play
The Plated City
Salem Kittredge and Other Stories
The Broughton House

PARK-STREET PAPERS

Park-Street Papers

By Bliss Perry

TOVT BIEN · OV RIEN

The Riverside Press

Boston and New York

Houghton Mifflin Company

1908

SECOND IMPRESSION

TO

GEORGE H. MIFFLIN

MAKER OF BEAUTIFUL BOOKS

WHOSE LOYALTY TO HIGH STANDARDS

HAS UPHELD

AT NO. 4 PARK STREET

THE GREAT TRADITIONS OF PUBLISHING

AND WHOSE KINDNESS OF HEART

HAS ENDEARED HIM

TO HIS ASSOCIATES

Preface

THE papers now gathered into this volume, in the author's tenth year of service as editor of *The Atlantic Monthly*, are concerned with the magazine itself, with its pleasant home in Park Street, and with some of the writers who have given distinction to its pages. Under the general title of "Atlantic Prologues" I have reprinted some of the brief Toastmaster addresses with which, in recent years, I have been in the habit of introducing each January number of the magazine. Although these informal addresses discuss primarily the surroundings and spirit of the Atlantic Monthly, they may also serve to suggest some of the constant problems involved in the art and mystery of magazine editing. It has happened that the centenaries of the births of several of the most famous early contributors to the Atlantic have fallen within the period of my own editorship. The essays upon Hawthorne, Longfellow, and Whittier are studies prompted by these anniversary occasions. The paper upon Thomas Bailey

Preface

Aldrich, one of the vivid and delightful figures in the already shadowy line of Atlantic editors, was written immediately after his death in 1907. I have also included in this volume, which begins and ends with the Atlantic, a paper prepared for the Fiftieth Anniversary number, in November, 1907, dealing with F. H. Underwood, whose share in founding the magazine has never received quite adequate recognition.

B. P.

CAMBRIDGE, 1908.

Contents

ATLANTIC PROLOGUES

Number 4 Park Street

In the days before the souvenir postal card was employed to advertise every corner of the globe, it was always a pleasure to receive one of those tinted cards decorated with a sprawling picture of some German town, and bearing a word of hearty German greeting. *Gruss aus Heidelberg!* Or perhaps it was Jena, Munich, or Nuremberg that furnished the cheap little picture and friendly word that wished you welfare and good cheer. How that pleasant custom warmed one's heart toward the far-away, thrifty city, and the old friends and old ways! It refreshed one's memory better than any Baedeker, — that simple, big-chested, deep-throated word *Gruss!* And it emboldens the Atlantic's Toastmaster to voice in similar fashion the salutation of the magazine to its readers. Greeting, Cheerful Readers all! Let it be a greeting from Number 4 Park Street.

[3]

cious sunny room on a level with the elm-
tops. Once, at least, in its century-old history,
the room was the chamber of a bride. Here are
her initials, scratched upon the window-pane
with her ring, while she was waiting for the car-
riage to bear her to the church, more than forty
years ago. Later, it was the nest of a quaint
old pair of abolitionists, who, when the days of
their warfare were accomplished, here lived out
their lives in peace. Many pairs of eyes have
gazed into the plain marble fireplace, or out
across the treetops toward the open country,
without leaving behind them any memory or
sign. The walls of the room now speak of literary associations merely. They are hung with
portraits of former editors, and with autograph
manuscripts of the brilliant group of writers
who gave to the Atlantic its early fame. Yet
some human quality other than literary, some
touch of the ardor, the curiosity, the silent en-
durance of the men and women who have lived
within the stout brick walls of Number 4, may
still be present here, secretly fashioning the fortunes of the Atlantic of to-day.

Does this lurking *genius loci* affect the magazine, whether its conductors will or no? Take,

for instance, the view from these sunny windows. They look down upon the mild activities of Park Street, to the left upon the black lines of people streaming in and out of the Subway, in front toward the Common with its fountain that never flows and its Frog Pond gleaming through the elms, and to the right toward the monument to Colonel Robert Gould Shaw. Is all this fairly typical of American life,—its work and play, its resourcefulness and its carelessness, its tolerant respect for the past, its posthumous honors gladly paid to the leaders of forlorn hopes? Or is it merely a view of Boston, something local, provincial; and our outlook from the Park Street windows, instead of summarizing and symbolizing the American, the human spectacle, is it only "Frogpondium"— as the scoffers have dubbed it — after all?

It is an interesting question, and one which the readers of the magazine must answer for themselves. Very likely they can determine, better than any observer stationed at Number 4 Park Street, whether the Atlantic is provincial or national. Or rather, since every magazine is necessarily provincial in some sort, it is for them to say whether the Atlantic's provincialism is of that honest kind which is rooted in the soil, and hence is truly representative of and contributory to the national life.

Certain it is, on the one hand, that the Atlantic has always been peculiarly identified with Boston. "Our Boston magazine," Emerson called it somewhat proudly, shortly after the first number was published. "Of Boston, Bostonese," wrote a New Orleans critic the other day, — "full of visionary ideals, impressed by a certain dogmatic scholarship, and when not riding any one of its literary hobbies, profoundly intellectual." Other contemporary notices are not always so gracious in their identification of Bostonian characteristics with the traits of the Atlantic. The faithful clipping bureaus furnish a choice collection of denunciatory epithets, aimed partly at Boston, partly at Number 4 Park Street, whenever the politics and philosophy of the magazine are not such as our journalistic friends approve.

Yet neither the original founders of the Atlantic Monthly, nor any of its conductors, have ever purposed to make it an organ of Bostonian or New England opinion. Its aim from the first has been national. It has striven to give expression to the best thought of the whole country, and an examination of the long rows of its bound volumes is the most convincing evidence of the cosmopolitan character of its articles. In the earlier years of its existence, it is true that the majority of the best-known American writers were living within twenty-five miles of the Massachusetts State House. These authors, by reason of their unsigned, but easily recognized contributions, gave the magazine the reputation which it has been fortunate enough to maintain. But before the Civil War was over, the number of different writers for the Atlantic had greatly increased, and the "red-eyed men"—as Emerson called them—who examined the manuscripts which were submitted to it found themselves struggling, like their successors to-day, with a flood of blackened paper from every quarter of the country. There is no longer any "literary centre" in America. The publishing centre is New York, but our writers cannot now be "rounded up" in the old easy fashion. All of the greater American magazines disclaim a special "sphere of influence." They pride themselves upon their national quality, and fear the provincial note.

Park-Street Papers

The publishers of many periodicals have reasoned that the readiest way of acquiring the air of cosmopolitanism is to give their magazine the imprint of the commercial capital of the country. Witness the opinion of that shrewdest of prospectus-makers, Edgar Allan Poe. In the last year of his life he was invited by a Mr. E. H. N. Patterson to become the editor of a new magazine. In Mr. Patterson's judgment, "The Boston Reviewers are, generally, too much affected by local prejudices to give impartial criticisms; the Philadelphia magazines have become mere monthly bulletins for booksellers." He therefore proposes to found, under Poe's editorship, an "influential periodical" at Oquawka, Ill. "Oquawka," he admits, "is comparatively an unimportant point, but I think that such being the case would not injure at all the circulation of the magazine. . . . Here I can enjoy every mail advantage that I could at St. Louis, being but thirty hours' travel from that city, and being situated immediately upon the Mississippi, with daily connection with the Northern Canal and St. Louis, and directly upon the great daily mail line from the East, through Pennsylvania,

[10]

Ohio, and Indiana." This is very charming.
But Poe, while assenting to the proposal, and
incidentally borrowing from his new publisher
fifty dollars on account, balks at that ominous
word Oquawka. "I submit to you," he replies,
"whether it be not possible to put on our title-
page *Published simultaneously at New York and
St. Louis*—or something equivalent."

There speaks, with unashamed frankness,
your seasoned editor and author. To live in
Oquawka, and yet to convey the impression
of being "Published simultaneously at New
York"! What a dream it is! And how it makes
cowards of us all! The Atlantic, at least, owns
to its Oquawka; it puts "4 Park Street, Boston" in bold-faced type upon its cover, and
prints "New York" in diminutive italics.

But rusticity will betray itself; your man
from the provinces remains a provincial to the
end. Very possibly that lurking *genius loci*
controls the Atlantic, and makes it, not an All-
American, as one would like to think it, but
only a Boston magazine. In vain, perhaps,
does it summon men reared in Ohio, North
Carolina, or New York to become its editors;
in vain does it select its writers from every state

in the Union. Doubtless the influence of the old
brick mansion, in the pleasant provincial street,
pervades, like a subtle spell, every editorial act
of invitation, acceptance, or rejection. One cannot escape it even by that simple device of putting a few hundred miles between oneself and
one's desk. Number 4 Park Street still keeps
its viewless, immitigable grip upon the fleeing
editor. It gives him what the Atlantic's prosperous Christian Scientist neighbors call "absent treatment." In vain does he mingle with
"common fowlers, tobacco-takers, and other
persons who can give no good account of how
they spend their time"; in vain does he seat
himself at noontide upon some stump in the
North Country, light an innocent pipe, and
count the fish in his basket. Telegrams find
their way through; the very birds of the air
keep twittering of articles; Park Street and
"the traditions of the Atlantic" are with him
still. The skies change, but not that habit of
trying all things — even the trout in one's basket — by the test of "availability." It is a case
of *cælum non animum*.

Well, so let it be! Here is the Atlantic for
better or worse, — stamped ineffaceably, it may

[12]

be, with the characteristics of its physical environment. An up-to-date journal has just remarked that "the venerable Park Street publication has bats in its belfry." Very likely. But is not its habitation just back of the steeple of Park Street Church? Do not its rear windows look out upon a graveyard, and its front windows upon that sorriest symbol of New England sterility, a fountain which has long since forgotten how to flow? Is a mere magazine to be luckier than the New Englander himself? He too, poor soul, tries to be friendly with all the world, but he cannot learn that trick of the "glad hand," so easily acquired elsewhere. He would like to be hospitable, but somehow his fountains do not spontaneously bubble with oil and wine. By nature he is no hater of his kind, and yet Heaven has placed him in a climate best described by Cotton Mather: "*New England*, a country where splenetic Maladies are prevailing and pernicious, perhaps above any other, hath afforded numberless instances, of even pious people, who have contracted these *Melancholy Indispositions*, which have unhinged them from all service or comfort; yea, not a few persons have been hurried thereby to lay

[13]

Violent Hands upon themselves at the last. These are among the *unsearchable Judgments* of God."

If the Atlantic shares these inexplicable defects of the New England qualities, will not its readers accept its greetings none the less? For the Atlantic, upon the word of the Toastmaster, means well. Jesting aside, it is mightily proud of its own little corner of the world. It has a stubborn affection for the simple ways of the older American life. It loves the memory of the gentlemen and scholars and men of letters who once frequented Park Street. It is housed more happily in the ancient Quincy mansion than in any tall office-building of Gath or Askelon. The skyscraper has not yet become the sacred emblem of America, nor has it been proved that the vortex of the mob is the best place wherein to observe and comment upon the growth of our civilization. Park Street is somewhat apart from the insane whirl which is miscalled "progress." Yet the magazine published at Number 4 somehow made a place for itself before the days of "commercial invasions" and "world records" and "Anglo-Saxon domination"; and it will continue to prosper long after the fads of the present hour have given place to others. If ghosts of dead abolitionists still haunt its sanctum, they are honest ghosts, and will do the editorial policy no harm. And if the outlook from its windows is only upon Boston Common instead of upon one of the great arteries of the world's trade, here, nevertheless, upon the corner of that Common, is something which far more than makes amends. No magazine that has the Shaw Memorial before its windows can be quite indifferent to human liberty, or be persuaded that commercial supremacy is the noblest ideal of an American citizen.

Catering for the Public

THE best that may be said for Thoreau's regimen of beans is, not that that immortal diet was merely wholesome or cheap, or even that it was transmuted into delightful literature, — but that Thoreau liked it. He was catering for himself and to himself. When Byron came of age, he provided the conventional roast ox and ale for his tenants in honor of his majority, and then dined alone upon his favorite delicacy, eggs and bacon. He catered for his public first, and to himself afterwards. But the only editors who permit themselves such solitary luxury of personal indulgence are the young men who own, write, and print the queer little 5×7 magazines with still queerer names. They give no hostages to fortune except paper, printer's ink, and time. If you would seek a better analogy to the real editorial function, follow some excellent citizen of Baltimore, or of a foreign city where marketing bears as yet no social stigma, as he journeys to the public market, with basket upon his careful arm, intent upon selecting a dinner for his family.

Observe him. For all his apparent leisureliness of manner, the good gentleman is carrying the burden of a theory. He has certain convictions, more or less definite, about desirable combinations of food and drink. Convention, which is only common sense deposited for long periods upon the reluctant mind of our species, has dictated to him some rude outline of a bill of fare. He has individual partialities of taste, but he has also tolerably distinct ideas of what is possible for his purse. Terrapin and champagne must be for high days only. Our worthy householder has also some fixed notions as to what is best for his family. They will thrive better, he knows, upon honest soups and roasts than upon cocktails and *éclairs*. Thus, as he makes his way from stall to stall, does he select, from the countless appetizing things displayed, the material for a foreordained dinner. He buys it, precisely as he would gather harmoniously colored flowers for a bouquet, and tucking it into that ample basket, takes it home in all innocence of heart. It is his affair, after all. If he and his family like what is purchased, well and good, provided their tastes do not become a public scandal, or their cookery grow too menacing to their neighbors' peace of mind. It is a simple matter, this catering for a family table, though not quite so simple as Thoreau's beans or Byron's eggs and bacon. But where is the analogy to editing a magazine? Is it so cunningly hidden away in this image of the householder that one cannot find it at all?

"Patience a moment," — to quote the most impatient of poets. We are getting "warm," as the children say, and in a minute more we shall discover our complete and archetypal editor. He is foreshadowed in the market-haunting householder, but he *is* — the being who keeps boarders.

Is it not so? The boarding-house keeper is no vulgar caterer to the public in general. He leaves that art to the yellow journal and the corner saloon. But he does cater for that portion of the public who have done him the honor to become his guests. Individual dietary theory may still lurk in his imagination, but it must not be over-indulged. His own favorite beans or

eggs and bacon will be too monotonous for his
boarders. The family responsibilities of the
householder linger in him, too; he must not
poison his boarders, or subtly undermine their
faith in human nature. Yet he has his weekly
or monthly bills to meet, and he can meet them
only by pleasing his patrons. Not what his
boarders ought to like, if they would grow truly
fat and wise and good, but what they do like,
gradually comes to affect the policy of even the
most stubborn-souled Provider.

The Toastmaster wonders if any readers of
the Atlantic recall the once famous *pension* in
Paris, kept by M. Alphonse Doucette, "for-
merly professor at Lyons"? It was known in
the Anglo-American colonies, from one end of
Europe to the other, as the *pension des violettes*,
—spoken with a smile. Yes, one smiled at M.
Doucette's amiable vagaries, but one kept on
going there, and paying a whole franc more a
day than was charged at any *pension* of its class
in Paris. For, as every one hastened to explain,
it was really an admirably kept establishment,
—and then, there were the violets! Every night
at dinner, in season or out of season, there was
a tiny boutonnière of them for each gentleman,

and a corsage bouquet of violets was laid by each
lady's plate. And Monsieur himself always sat
at the head of the table and addressed his varie-
gated company with the most incessant and
exquisite drollery. Only a franc more than was
charged at the commonplace *pensions,* and all
those violets thrown in!

It happened that the Toastmaster returned
to the Pension Doucette very late one night,
after witnessing a most dreary seven-act tragedy
at the Français. In the little office off the dining-
room sat M. Doucette in his shirt-sleeves, drink-
ing sugared water, and looking more tragic than
Mounet-Sully at his worst. Something had
gone wrong. It was a trivial matter enough, but
the former professor at Lyons opened his whole
heart. Never before or since — save once in
a Vermont woodshed on a Sunday morning,
when his host was morosely freezing the ice
cream for dinner and imparting with each slow
turn of the crank some darkly pessimistic gen-
eralization on the subject of summer boarders
— has the Toastmaster seen deeper into the
Caterer's professional soul. Oh, the sorrows of
trying to hold the fickle taste of English and
American visitors in Paris!

"But there are the violets," I ventured.

"The violets!" M. Doucette spread his palms.

A ghastly suspicion dawned upon me. Was his love for violets only a pretense?

"I loathe violets!" he broke out. "*À bas les violettes!* The odor and the sight of them are nauseating to me. But it is too late. If I were to give up the violets, I should lose my trademark, my prestige, my clientele. My pensionnaires *expect* violets!"

I saw the trap he had laid for himself. And, oddly enough, my thoughts wandered to the veteran editor of a famous magazine, who was once discussing two sonnets by the same poet. He had accepted one and rejected the other; and now he was praising the one he had returned.

"But it was the other which you printed!" exclaimed his puzzled auditor.

"Oh, that was my choice for the magazine, certainly; but personally—" And he waved his cigar stub in a parabola that opened up infinite distances of perspective into the editorial consciousness. Was it possible that he, too, loathed his violets?

And yet, why not? Not to speak it profanely, does anybody suppose that Mr. Munsey's favorite reading is the Munsey Storiettes?
Does "the sound of the swashbuckler swashing on his buckler" seem less humorous to the
editors who encourage it than it does to Mr.
Howells, who has laid aside his editorial armor
and can smile at the weaknesses of his former
fellow warriors? Do the peaceful editors of the
"Outlook" really thrill with those stern praises
of fighting men and fighting machines which
adorn its secularized pages? Or does the talented conductor of the "Ladies' Home Journal" really . . . No, he cannot. As the Toastmaster makes these too daring interrogations,
it seems to him that he perceives a faint odor
of violets, — not the shy flower of the woodside,
but the brazen-faced, tightly laced boutonnière
of the pavement, — in a word, the violet of
commerce.

That single glimpse of M. Doucette in his
shirt-sleeves and in his despondency ought not
to obliterate the memory of a hundred nights
when, clothed in proper evening attire, he
reigned gloriously over his long table-full of

guests, giving and receiving pleasure. When
all is going well, catering has its innocent delights and its honest satisfactions. To invent a
new dish, or to serve an old one with recognized skill, is to share at once the artist's joy
and the bourgeois's complacency. Yet having
once beheld the confidential shirt-sleeves, one
is thenceforward subtly aware of them, hidden
though they be for another hundred nights by
the dress coat. They are there, those shirt-
sleeves of the Caterer, and his workaday responsibilities are inescapable. In vain does Sir
Leslie Stephen, in one of those papers which
not long ago charmed the Atlantic's readers,
blithely assert that an editor "only vouches
for the readability of the article, not for the
correctness of the opinions expressed." It
is a millennial dream. It asks too much of
human nature. Shall the Toastmaster dare to
say, "My dear guests, I am no mycologist.
This dish may be toadstool or mushroom for
all I know, but I assure you that the odor is
appetizing"?

Alas, it is true that he is no mycologist; he
prints every month a dozen articles on topics
concerning which he knows nothing, as well as

a half-dozen more whose views of politics and society and criticism are the very opposite of his own. He vouches for their readability, that is all,—and sometimes this is quite enough to take upon his conscience. But the public is shrewdly suspicious of this happy impartiality of ignorance. It keeps reminding the Toast-master that he is Caterer too; that he has the responsibility of buying the provisions in the open market as well as merely arranging them on the table and announcing the bill of fare.

In one sense, the public is quite right. Some one must take the responsibility of decision. But the public sometimes forgets how the Caterer must make up in faith what he lacks in special knowledge. He depends upon the honesty of the marketmen, the producers. This confidence is rarely betrayed. M. Doucette would have died of shame, no doubt, if he had really served toadstools to his trusting company. Yet it never happened. His mushrooms were always mushrooms. It is the contributors to a magazine like the Atlantic who maintain, after all, the fine traditions of the institution. For purposes of convenience, it is assumed that the editor knows what he is purchasing. In reality, he is only exercising faith in writers who know what they are writing, and whose views — strange as it may seem! — may be worth consideration even if they do not harmonize with his own. The monthly table of contents is neither more nor less than such a confession of faith. It cannot be made without a certain hardihood. In camp, when it is your week to cook, you can always enjoy the luxury of finding fault with the man who laid in the supplies: he should have bought more bacon or a different brand of coffee, and why did he forget the onions? Even the suave conductor of the dining-car, who presents you with a menu which requests explicit criticism of meals and service, can shrug his shoulders and explain that he did not buy that steak himself. But here in the magazine world there is no shuffling. Month by month what is in the larder comes on to the table, and if it is mouldy or tough or raw the Toastmaster cannot blame the Caterer, for he is both in one: Dr. Jekyll and Mr. Hyde, the red slayer and the slain.

Who is there that can tell, after all, precisely how to please even the most indulgent of publics? The editors of the Atlantic have always

been drafted from the ranks of its contributors;
mere contributors, who once inclosed stamps
for the return of manuscript and waited and
wondered if it would prove "magazinable."
How can such a one, drawn in a moment, like
Browning's conscript,

" From the safe glad rear to the dreadful van,"

pretend that he has been invested with infalli-
bility? "I am fain to think it vivacious," wrote
Lowell of a certain Contributor's Club which
he was submitting to the editor in 1890, nearly
thirty years after his own editorship closed,
"but if your judgment verify my fears, don't
scruple to return it. I can easily make other
disposition of it, or at worst there is always the
waste-basket." His Club was accepted, in spite
of Lowell's fears, — and, as it happened, it was
his last contribution to the magazine. But
whenever an author's manuscript carries the
bunker of the editor's judgment, there remains
a far more formidable hazard still, namely, the
unknown taste of the public.

Who really understands it? Did not Emerson, that most unmercenary of editors, accept
for the "Dial," *pro honoris causa* and with a

sinking heart, that article of Theodore Parker's
on the Reverend John Pierpont, which nevertheless, to Emerson's astonishment, sold out
the entire edition? Did not Coleridge, an equally
unworldly member of the guild, lose five hundred subscribers to the ill-starred "Watchman"
on the publication of the very second number,
by "a censurable application of a text from
Isaiah as its motto"?

Of one thing only may the editor be sure. No
matter what dish he serves, some one at the
table will be positive that it ought not to have
been brought on at all, or that it should have
been cooked very differently. If the Atlantic
has dispatched a representative to Borrioboola
Gha to report upon the condition of blankets-
and-top-boots in that unhappy country, some
correspondent will turn up, as soon as the article is printed, to prove that he himself was the
sole originator of the blankets-and-top-boots
idea, and that the Atlantic has misrepresented
the blessed work now going forward there. May
he not have ample space in the next number
to reply? Well, very likely he ought to have
it. But the unlucky editor, puzzling at that
moment over the problem of finding space in

the issue three months hence, thinks with a
sigh of M. Doucette's *pension*. For at those
long table-d'hôte dinners no one was expected
to care for every course; if you allowed a dish
to pass or left it barely tasted, you must for that
very reason talk the more agreeably with your
neighbor; and if individual clamor over some
unfortunate concoction reached the quick ear
of M. Doucette, with what infinite ease and wit
did he offer the critic the honor of planning and
preparing the next meal in person, — an invitation which was somehow never accepted. Besides, as M. Doucette used sometimes to hint,
when flushed with his success, if one did not
like the *pension des violettes*, there were plenty
of other *pensions* across the way, eager for patronage.

Is all this too intimate a survey of the editorial pantry and kitchen? Pray consider it
nothing more than the shirt-sleeved conversation of that garrulous M. Doucette, provoked
into real confidence by an unusual hour. Forget, if you will, the unskilled service, and remember that market-place and kitchen are as
yet imperfect places in an imperfect, although

improvable and improving world. And be tolerant of the violets, purchased with such secret anxiety of heart, and laid by each plate with such grace as Park Street may afford.

The Cheerless Reader

ONE of the most genial of Atlantic essayists has lamented the disappearance of the Gentle Reader. Can it be possible that the Cheerful Reader is disappearing, too? One is loath to believe it; for if the Gentle Reader and the Cheerful Reader are both to vanish, and magazines are to be edited—as Dr. Crothers hinted —for the benefit of the Intelligent Reading Public merely, the world of periodical litera- ture will be a dismal world indeed. Yet if one were to judge from those Letters to the Editor, which the New York "Sun," for instance, prints, and the Atlantic, for another instance, does not print, the quality of cheerfulness is nowadays sadly strained. What streams of sor- rowful correspondence are directed to 4 Park Street after each issue of this magazine! And so few of them seem to flow from the pen of the Cheerful Reader! Perhaps the Cheerful Reader is busy earning his living,—too busy to write. It may be that it is only the Cheerless Persons who have leisure to take their pens in hand and "write to the editor."

If the Atlantic Monthly were a "repository"; if it confined itself to the discussion of Roman antiquities, or the sonnets of Wordsworth, or the planting of the colony of Massachusetts Bay, none but the specialists would concern themselves with the opinions expressed in its pages. But it happens to be particularly interested in this present world; curious about the actual condition of politics and society, of science and commerce, of art and literature. Above all, it is engrossed with the lives of the men and women who are making America what it is and is to be. The Atlantic is fortunate enough to command the services of many writers who have something to say upon these great and perplexing topics of human interest. It is not to be expected that they will agree with one another; perhaps they will not even, in successive articles, agree with themselves. Does the Atlantic print a clever woman's criticism of that useful institution the Kindergarten, straightway there arrive protesting letters from more Kindergart-

ners than it innocently supposed the whole
world could contain. When it allowed a distinguished college president to make a casual
remark about the unchanging curriculum of
Jesuit schools, there came a furious chorus from
various Jesuit contemporaries (some of them,
it is true, winking cordially, meanwhile, as if to
remind one of the Pickwickian flavor of the controversy!): "Why is your contemptible publication Anti-Catholic?" Alas! only a few months
before, when Mr. H. D. Sedgwick had given just
praise to the Roman Church in certain matters,
there was a similar chorus from many Protestant contemporaries, who announced their vo-
ciferant grief that the Atlantic had gone over to
Rome. Then it had been the turn of the Cath-
olic letter-writers to pose as Lifelong Readers.
But, queerly enough, a few months later still,
when Mr. Sedgwick made an Italian journey,
and described a station-master who had unquestionably had a bad dinner, and who was low in
his mind and spoke pessimistically of the Pope,
behold these same Lifelong Readers terminat-
ing their subscriptions, and writing mournfully
that they could not longer support such a bit-
terly sectarian publication as the Atlantic.

A more recent example of the uneven distribution of a sense of humor among Atlantic readers was the commotion caused by Mr. Eugene Wood's paper on Mrs. Eddy's literary style. Pathetic as it may seem to announce the fact now, this article was supposed to be humorous; its examination of some of the foibles of the Foundress was to be interpreted in the spirit of Stevenson's smiling paper on "John Knox and his Relations to Women." But alas! the able-bodied letter-writers of the Christian Scientist faith did not seem to know their Stevenson; and to all Earnest Persons in that curious organization the Atlantic expresses its regret that any of Mr. Wood's sallies should have given pain.

It is probable, however, that sectarians, sectionalists, and partisans of every hue will continue to peruse their Atlantic with sorrow, or at least sufficient sorrow for epistolary purposes. One's own hobby horse gets roughly shouldered to one side, on the broad highway of the world. Where opinions are unfettered and allowed frank expression, some truths will be uttered more wholesome than flattering to one's private views. John Doe may like the Atlantic,—

Heaven bless him!—but if he prefer to write
his name, like a story title, John Doe, Prohibi-
tionist, or John Doe, Baptist or Anabaptist,
Vivisectionist or Anti-Vivisectionist, Suffragist
or Anti-Suffragist, he will often discover that
the wrong magazine has been sent to his address.
If people insist upon regarding themselves primarily, not as human beings, but as members of
some organization ending with *ist* or *er* or *an*,
then the weekly or monthly organ of their particular faction will furnish them with far more
congenial reading than the Atlantic. The Gentle
Reader, declares Dr. Crothers in the essay already mentioned, is the reader who "has no
ulterior aims." Precisely. If your chief purpose
in taking a magazine is to find arguments for
your favorite "cause," you are in a parlous state.
You are in danger of evolving from a merely
Earnest Person into a Cheerless Person.

The Comic Spirit has whips for such. Not
all of them are punished as neatly as that Earnest Southerner who complained of a "color-
line" story in the Atlantic, "Why can't you
Northerners be decent?" only to learn that the
author of the story was a native of his own
county; or that Laudator Temporis Acti who

lately found fault with the "silly, ignorant twaddle" of a certain article in the Contributors' Club, which, he averred, would never have been printed in the good old days of Mr. Aldrich or Mr. Howells — and which, as the Comic Spirit would have it, was actually written by the faultless pen of Mr. Aldrich himself!

To have no "ulterior aims"! That is a counsel of perfection for reader and editor alike, and the Atlantic confesses that it would like to be thought to have no ulterior aims, except the pleasure and profit of its subscribers. Not one of its genuine Lifelong Readers will accuse it of dilettanteism, of treating the vital topics of the day with indifference. James Russell Lowell, who, in the words of Mr. Scudder's recent Life, "gave the Atlantic a character it has ever since maintained," was no Gallio. But neither was he a Cheerless Person. It is true that from the day on which he assumed the editorship the magazine was held stanchly to certain tenets: as, for instance, to take but a single example, the belief that equality of political privileges in America should not be affected by considerations of race or religion. Yet it has given the

freedom of its pages to a good many writers who
held quite the opposite view. It has been edited
for men and women genuinely curious about
affairs, politics, literature, human society. It is
not preoccupied with the claims of any particular sect or party or philosophy. "Thought
men" and "fact men," theorizers and workers,
have alike addressed its readers, provided they
had something magazinable to say, and could
say it in an interesting fashion. To imagine that
the contributors to such a magazine will always
agree with the editor, or please all the readers,
or indeed any reader in all his moods and opinions and convictions, is to hold a singularly
parochial view of periodical literature. It is only
your worthy rustic who wants nothing "in the
paper" which he does not already believe. Unless his political or religious opinions, derived
largely from it, are constantly reflected in it, he
will — as the saying used to be — "stop the
Tribune"!

The ideal magazine-reading mood — is it
not? — is that of well-bred people listening to
the after-dinner conversation in public which
has happily succeeded after-dinner "oratory."
No matter how varied and attractive the pro-

gramme of addresses may be, no guest will be
thrilled by every speaker. You are perhaps
fortunate if you are thrilled at all! But if the
speeches are tolerably short, and represent a
wide range of opinion, and are cleverly phrased,
one may be expected to listen without making
oneself conspicuous by either protest or ap-
plause. No man, perhaps, makes precisely the
speech you would like to hear. He may hurt
somebody's feelings, — possibly your own.
This may be inevitable, or merely the result of
inadvertency; or it may be the fault of the
Toastmaster, who ought to have warned the
speaker that So-and-So was at the banquet, and
that certain things had better be left unsaid. A
quicker-witted Toastmaster, for example, might
have nudged Mr. Eugene Wood under the
table, by way of friendly warning that the exact
number of Mrs. Eddy's marriages was a vex-
atious theme to certain persons who had purchased dinner-tickets, and that in any case it had
nothing to do (save as bearing upon that lady's
ripeness of experience) with the subject of her
literary style.

For the magazine means to spread each
month a hospitable board, and to draw around

it many men of many minds. Mr. Roosevelt and Mr. Washington have both sat there, and we hope that both men will honor the Atlantic many times again, by contributing their quota to its wit and wisdom. People who do not like good company, who prefer to dine exclusively with Cheerless Persons of Their Own Sort, are not under the slightest obligation to attend. Our "mahogany tree" has to be made longer, month by month, to accommodate the new guests that wish to mingle with the old. To add more leaves to such an infinitely extensible dining-table is, of course, a pleasure. Yet it will do no harm to sit closer, too, with an amiable disposition to be pleased, if possible, with one's fellow guests, and to make all needful allowance for a most fallible Toastmaster.

"A Readable Proposition"

ONCE more the Toastmaster rises to his feet, to offer greetings to the guests of the Atlantic. The table has become a long one, and the faces turned momentarily toward the Toastmaster are mainly those of Cheerful Readers. If any are secretly bored or rebellious at the bill of fare, they seem, at this kindly instant, gracious enough not to betray it. Most of them, as the Toastmaster fancies, — for he is not sufficiently keen-sighted to see to the end of such a table, and makes many a mistake in consequence! — exhibit a tolerant willingness to be either edified or amused. And, indeed, both edification and amusement await them, the Toastmaster believes, as soon as his own little speech is over.

He chooses his text from one of those plain-spoken letters which evince the interest taken in the Atlantic by persons who have parted with their four dollars a year, and who keep, as they should, a sharp eye upon their investment. The letter is from a Wyoming sheep-herder, and here is one of its most pleasing sentences: " I would like you to know that you have one subscriber who has no kick coming, and who thinks the Atlantic is a readable proposition all right."

May the clear Wyoming sky long smile upon this solitary sheep-herder! May his flocks increase, and his vocabulary remain unspoiled! He has a discriminating taste. Or is it merely the liberal Western air which prompts him to utter what many other subscribers silently believe? After all, one can never tell who is going to like the gallant old magazine. The Toastmaster finds himself scrutinizing, with perhaps too frank an admiration, the persons who have the excellent habit of reading the Atlantic in hotels and trains and electric cars. A pretty girl never seems so pretty, to him, as when she is carrying that bit of dull orange color; and the most prosaic middle-aged searcher after truth never appears in such imminent prospect of a radiant discovery as when cutting the Atlantic's uncut leaves. He remembers sitting once in an overland train as it coasted down the slope of the Sierras through the Bret Harte country.

"A Readable Proposition"

He was thinking of those brilliant early stories
of Harte's which the Atlantic published, and
was watching gloomily, all the while, a certain
bishop who was reading the "Smart Set." The
train pulled up at a little station, and a muddy-
trousered miner, looking for all the world like
Kentuck, entered the car, stumbled past the
comfortably extended legs of the bishop, and
seating himself at the magazine table, promptly
selected the Atlantic Monthly. The Toastmaster grew cheerful at once. He began to think
of cogent reasons why the good bishop should
prefer the "Smart Set," and nothing could
have persuaded him that the miner was not a
Superior Person.

The odd thing is that it is impossible to guess
where these Superior Persons are to be found.
It is an illuminating experience to examine the
Atlantic's subscription list in some city or town
which happens to be well known to the investi-
gator. To subscribe to this magazine is apparently no longer — as it was once said to be in
certain newly settled communities — a sufficient
evidence of one's social standing. Many of the
Best People who would be expected to take it
evidently belong in the class who vaguely "see

all the magazines at the Club"; while the Superior Persons who actually pay the four dollars are often to be found in the side streets and hall-bedrooms and lonely farmhouses. Other magazines, it is believed, have had the same experience in endeavoring to discover the exact habitat of the reading class. It is such readers, in truth, who form our only real reading class in this country. If the Atlantic continues to interest them, year after year, it is not because the magazine is a badge of respectability, but simply because it is found to be "a readable proposition."

The dictionaries give the bare outline of that finely American term, "proposition," but they do not even hint at the warmth and coloring given to it on the lips of living men. What a wholesome, venturesome, tempting Americanism it is! It savors of something coming even if not yet arrived; of something alive and not yet dead and done with. It suggests, indeed, unlisted stocks and extra-hazardous enterprises, rather than the commonplace security of a three per cent government bond. Such a bond is well enough in its way, of course, but what is its appeal to the imagination, after all, when com-

pared with a " proposition "? The spirit of all
the beckoning future is in that word, and yet
with how deft a compliment does our Wyoming
friend apply it to the magazine, as if he had re-
alized upon his investment, and the potential
pleasure offered by his subscription were already
a known quantity!

With what an instinct, likewise, does the gentleman from Wyoming select his inevitable word
when he speaks of the Atlantic as a *readable*
proposition! "It is better to be dumb than not
to be understood," said the lively Giraldus Cam-
brensis, who was a born magazinist, although
of the twelfth century. When a magazine fails
to be readable, it is as if a man failed in honesty
or a woman in goodness. Its character is gone.
There are tons of respectable printed material
which is under no necessity of being readable:
such as Doctor's Dissertations, Presidential
Messages, books written in the jargon of some
special science, and journals devoted to some pet
ist or *ism* of the hour. Most unreadable of all
is the matter written with a painful effort to be
read by everybody. Witness the average Historical Romance of the season! Not long ago
the Toastmaster happened to overhear a wor-

thy nursemaid exchanging literary confidences with the cook, apropos of a historical novel which was then the best-selling book of the minute. "Sure it's a fine book," testified Maggie heartily, and then added, as if puzzled by her own ineptitude, "but somehow I ain't very far with it." Exactly. Neither was the Toastmaster very far with it. Between a book written to be sold by the hundred thousand and a book written to be put away in a drawer, like "Pride and Prejudice" and the first draft of "Waverley," it is tolerably easy to say which is the more likely to prove permanently readable.

A good many readers, and not all of them nursemaids, either, have been complaining that the poetry published in American magazines is unreadable, too. Perhaps they ought to say "verse" instead of "poetry," for it is obvious that most poets nowadays are not working at their trade. Some of them are dead, others have gone into politics or play-writing; but the silence of the majority can be accounted for only on the theory that the poets are out on a sympathetic strike. Who can blame them? Poor pay, long hours, an apathetic public, and thousands of verse-writers ready to take the poets' places

at any moment! The worst of it is that these
very "scabs"—the word is used in its stern
economic significance—are all bent upon producing "readable" verse. They not only continue to rhyme

. . . . youth
. . . . morning
. . . . truth
. . . . warning

as the Autocrat humorously complained in
these pages long ago, but they insist upon tell-
ing us all about their little emotions, with the
tiresome particularity of a dull sportsman who
persists in explaining just why he failed to bag
that last bird. Their mind to them a kingdom
is, and, as somebody has unkindly said of them,
the smaller the mind the greater appears the
kingdom. No wonder the public has grown
callous to all this counting of the pulses and
auscultation of the chest. The exploitation of
insignificant personalities, bent upon securing
publicity, makes verse as unreadable as the "society column" of a Sunday paper. No wonder
that so many real poets continue to stay out on
strike. But some day there will come along a
modern hero in the guise of a strapping strike-

breaker of a poet, who would rather work at his job than not, who, forgetting himself, believes that the world is a big world and a brave one, and who sings about it because he must, and not because he wants to make readable "copy." He will get all the patronage away from the clever verse-writers, and then the poets will begin to slink back, one by one, to ask for their old places. In the meantime the Atlantic tries to keep a sharp and welcoming eye upon anything that looks like a broad-shouldered strike-breaker sauntering down Park Street. Often it is deceived and finds that the new personage is only one more of those talented verse-writers, but still it keeps on watching.

What is it, after all, that makes a magazine readable? Must we not fall back upon the well-tested phrase, and say that "human interest" is the one essential quality? But the human interest must be real, and not assumed for revenue only. Two of the most uniformly readable newspapers in this country are the New York "Sun" and the "Springfield Republican." Neither can be read without wrath, or given up without a feeling that the world has grown duller. Both are vigorous, alert, and well written. They differ in their attitude toward most public questions; they differ in field, one being "metropolitan" and the other "provincial," — though which is the more truly provincial who is bold enough to say? — and there is a difference in personal style which may be detected in almost every sentence. Yet both, from the first line to the last, quicken one's curiosity, interest, knowledge, about human life. They manage to convey to the most indifferent reader a vivid sense of what people are thinking about, what they feel and really are.

It is this quality, — is it not? — which, making due allowance for differences in range, perspective, and literary method, should also characterize a monthly magazine. The Atlantic has many competitors. The more the better. Each of them fulfills some public service peculiar to itself, — even if it be only to serve as an "awful example." Each of them reaches many persons whom the Atlantic cannot reach without changing its character and aim. The colored illustrations of one, the unimpeachable innocuousness of another, the agility of a third in jumping to the majority side of every question, do not arouse the Atlantic's envy. It would like, indeed, to give its contributors a still ampler audience, because it believes that all of them have something to say which is worth listening to. But these opinions of its contributors are their own,—as the Toastmaster has pointed out more than once in his annual remarks,—and are not to be identified with whatever personal opinions may be held by the Atlantic's editors or publishers. Sydney Smith claimed that there were persons who would speak disrespectfully of the equator; and some writers for the Atlantic have been known to approach with a freedom bordering upon levity such topics as Emerson, the Kindergarten, the New England Hill Town, Sir Walter Scott, the Philippine Commission, Lincoln's Vocabulary, the Tariff, and Mr. Henry James. This list might even be extended. There are, alas, live wires attached to all live subjects as well as to some subjects that seem tolerably dead. The Atlantic has no Index of forbidden themes, and wishes all its writers to say what they think, subject to the general rules of after-dinner courtesy. But it does smile occasionally over this identification of supposed editorial opinion with the signed opinions of responsible contributors. If

[48]

an article appears in the Atlantic, it is because the
contribution seems, in the fallible judgment of
the Caterer, worth putting upon the table. If
the boarders do not like it, the blame must be
placed where it belongs. Probably the fault lies
with the Caterer, but it is barely possible that it
may lie, at times, with some prenatal or premil-
lennial prejudices of the boarders themselves.

Our "readable proposition," then, is the discussion from month to month, by many men
of many minds, of that American life which
intimately affects the destiny of us all. If one
wishes to study that life upon its external aspects, the advertising pages of any prosperous
magazine give a bewilderingly rich impression
of our material progress. There is scarcely a
single physical activity or luxury, from drawing
one's cold tub in the morning to setting the
burglar alarm at night, which is not pictured
and glorified upon these electrotyped pages.
But something in us keeps obstinately asking :—

"And afterwards, what else?"

For it makes little difference whether a man
speeds in his new automobile over the new
macadam to his new country house, — man and

machine and road and house exactly like the
advertisements!—or climbs wearily up to the
hall-bedroom again at the end of a day's work,
to console himself with a pipe and a book. Each
man must sit down at last with his old self;
with the old hopes, sorrows, dreams; with the
old will to "win out" somehow; with that inner
world, in short, which Literature interprets, and
no hint of which appears in the advertising
pages. A true mirror of life is what a literary
magazine aspires to be. But it ought to reflect
something deeper than the patented, nickel-
plated conveniences and triumphs of a material
civilization. It should also serve as a mirror for
the ardors and loyalties, the patriotism and the
growing world-consciousness of the American
people.

Any writer mistakes our people who does not
recognize their fundamental idealism. Some of
us inherit it from Puritan ancestors who were
such idealists, it is said, that they had to hold
on hard to the huckleberry bushes to keep from
being translated. Others of us have brought
hither a no less fine idealism, though it be the
product of an alien faith and an alien soil. But
it is everywhere in evidence, setting up popular

[50]

idols and pulling them down, blundering here
and righting a blunder there, questioning our
present social and economic machinery, em-
phasizing party lines when they stand for something real, smashing them when trickery grows
too apparent, and building everywhere with
restless energy a new America out of materials
that have never had time to grow old. Inn-
keepers abroad and advertising panels at home
unite in the declaration that "Americans want
the best." It is a good symptom, and it has a
lesson for the magazinist. Those periodicals
which are obtaining the widest reading are those
which present the most various, hopeful, and
full-blooded pictures of the men and the vital
forces that are daily creating for us a new world.
Never were our life and the life of the globe so
interesting. The magazine desires long to remain "a readable proposition." It surely will,
if it continues in its own way to reflect and interpret, as all literature somehow succeeds in
reflecting and interpreting, the fascination of
life itself.

Turning the Old Leaves

THERE is too much said at New Year's —
in the Toastmaster's opinion — about turning
over a new leaf. Are the old leaves all so badly
written that one must hasten to forget them?
Is the blank whiteness of the untouched page
more pleasant to the eye or more fortifying to
the will than those closely written, underlined,
untidy, but familiar pages which make up the
story of one's life? These pages of experience
turn so easily in the hand! They open by themselves to so many passages worth remembering.
Will the trim virgin pages of the New Year
yield anything really more desirable? Doubtless there may be finer bread than is made of
wheat, and a nobler fish than the salmon, and
a better book than "Henry Esmond," but we
shall be lucky if we find them during the next
twelve months.

No, this annual counsel to turn over a new

leaf is but a restless, dissatisfied injunction. One's old habits may not have been such bad habits, after all. Does the handwriting always improve with age and practice? Some of the old habits may be deemed actually good, even by the sharpest-visaged conscience that ever went peering about, like a meticulous housekeeper, on New Year's morning. And even if the old ways, hopes, and day's works were not all of the very first quality, the Toastmaster protests against that unmindful virtue that would turn them all outdoors at the end of December, to make room for the guests of the New Year. The new guests come, indeed, but the house seems empty.

Have any of the Atlantic's readers, in the course of one of those changes of residence so typical of our migratory race and epoch, ever sat perplexed before a packing-box, hesitating whether to keep or throw away a bundle of old cheque-books? Hesitation is dangerous. If you once begin to turn over the stubs of those cheques long since drawn and cashed, the moments slip by unheeded. What an odd summary of experience is chronicled in those names and dates and figures! They are abstracts of

duties and pleasures that had slipped quite
down between the cracks of memory, yet here
they are as fresh as yesterday's. Here are the
butcher, the baker, and the candlestick-maker,
with faces no longer blurred, for you, by dozens
of their successors. You smile at this stub, and
the next you turn hastily over; you find yourself angry still at the record of some ancient ex-
tortion on the part of plumber or tax-gatherer;
you look ruefully at the figures representing
some unwonted extravagance or folly; or you
catch yourself in the act of pious approbation
of some forgotten benevolence. That cheque,
at least, ought to have been larger! A curious
sense of reality takes possession of you, as you
scan these laconic entries. They recall so much.
The half-filled packing-box, the littered room,
the confused misery of migration, all shift into
dream-land; while you, through the magic
wrought by a few dusty, outlawed slips of paper,
seem to feel the touch of Life's very garment,
— it is all so real! A great historian once
sneered at that method of historical research
which scrutinizes mediæval wash-lists in the
hope of learning something about mediæval
men and women. If he had ever looked over his

own old cheque-books, he would have spared the sneer.

Some such intimate contact with the spirit of this magazine has the Toastmaster recently experienced, in turning the leaves of the earliest numbers. Those were cheque-books indeed! What rich accounts of wit, of poetry, and of scholarship to draw upon, and how liberal were the drafts! And the readers of that day, eager for intellectual pleasures, for new information, for moral stimulus, indorsed so promptly the cheques drawn by the contributors! To each subscriber there must have come the excited consciousness of a largesse up to the very limit of his capacity for enjoyment. There were dull contributions now and then, and doubtless there was an unappreciative reader here and there, but if the subscriber of fifty years ago did not, in the course of a twelve-month, have his money's worth of pleasure, it was not the fault of Dr. Holmes and Professor Lowell and the other capitalists of wit and learning. These Autocrats, Biglows, and other Olympians drew the cheques lavishly, and the Atlantic subscribers might cash them if they wished.

It is all recorded in those bound volumes

that stand upon the library shelves of so many of
the older generation of Atlantic readers. There
are the names and dates and subjects. Some of
them are still vital, still a part of our national
literature. Yet a large proportion of the pages
in those files must necessarily seem of outworn
value unless they are viewed as stubs in an old
cheque-book. So read by the curious or pious,
how full of significance they become for the interpretation of the last half-century of American
letters and American history! The fading, outlawed leaves are once more coin of the realm of
thought. Behind the dusty volumes rise troops
of eager readers,—applauding, questioning,
combative,—precisely like the subscribers of
to-day. For that matter, the Atlantic is im-
mensely proud that a long roll of names, first
inscribed in 1857, are still upon its subscription
lists. When two or three of this old guard take
pains to write and say that a current article is
good, the Toastmaster believes them. Only the
other day one of these valiant souls wrote that
she had just finished reading every volume from
the beginning, except for a period of two years,
when the magazine was unaccountably dull!
The Toastmaster, who has the curiosity but not

the courage to ask the date of those two lean years, congratulates his correspondent upon possessing the alchemy of an imagination which brings the old days back and still hears the old voices speaking with undiminished charm.

To most of us, lacking as we do that evoking imagination, the secret of literary vitality seems baffling, incommunicable. Why should it be that one poem or story, printed for good "journalistic" reasons in 1857, should be recognized a half-century later as "literature," while its companion pieces have utterly vanished from memory? We have our private guesses, of course, and our triumphant public demonstrations of the presence of this or that antiseptic quality in the piece in question. But the explanations do not wholly explain. It is only the listening imagination that can divine the mystery, and distinguish the immortal from the transient voices.

In one sense, indeed, the changes wrought by the last half-century are apparent to the most careless eye that glances over those bound volumes of which we have been speaking. Since that panic year of 1857 — darkened by financial disaster and by the ever-nearing conflict over slavery — what political, social, and commercial developments have altered the material aspect of the United States! The magazine writers who have striven to interpret these changes have been dealing with a shifting world. It is like photographing from a raft the waves of the sea. The writers themselves have often altered their convictions and purpose; they have gained or lost in talent or inspiration. Unknown to themselves, the magazine-reading public has reassessed them, decade after decade, at a lower, or perhaps at a higher figure. That public itself is constantly dropping away, and is as constantly renewed. It is necessarily fickle in its attachments, given to swift enthusiasms and long forgetfulness. "Who was that young fellow who went up and came down again like a rocket?" asked Frank Stockton of the Toastmaster, a year or two after "The Red Badge of Courage" had been published; "was it *William* Crane?" "Stephen," corrected the Toastmaster. There was a whimsical smile upon Stockton's dark, gentle, tired face, as if he meant to hint that all our little rockets will come down in time. And no doubt most of them do. There are already persons who ask "who was Frank Stockton?" and the Toastmaster remembers dining at an American table with an accomplished and cultivated company, not one of whom, as it turned out, had ever read "Vanity Fair."

Amid all this impermanence, it is no wonder that even a casual scrutiny of the Atlantic files should reveal editorial inconsistencies and partialities of vision. Here is the dusty record of unskillful literary prophecies, of Presidential "booms" that came to nothing, of social tendencies that sloped, as it proved, in unsuspected directions, and of Utopian rearrangements that still await the fit hour and the man. Some of the intrenched political and social abuses against which the Atlantic's writers have turned their heaviest guns seem as stoutly intrenched as ever, and likely to afford splendid shooting for another half-century. Many of the "big" articles which were expected to batter down these forts of folly are now recognized by the very office-boys as ill-aimed or premature. The best editorial devices for winning and holding readers often seem, in the retrospect, so illogical and naïve! Tramping through the Belgian Dinant one rainy evening last summer, the Toastmaster halted in admiration before the tent of

[59]

some strolling French players, who were winning a harvest at a peasants' fair. The buxom
mother of the family, perched, short-skirted
and merry-eyed, upon a platform in front of
the tent, harangued her audience of Ardennes
peasants upon the merits of the representation
that was about to be given. The oldest boy
blew painfully at a bugle, while a younger boy
—between bites of an apple—rang a brass bell.
The half-grown daughter shook a tambourine
coquettishly under the noses of the village
youth. The father sold the admission tickets.
And what was the programme that was pack-
ing the tent with honest Ardennes folk, at fifteen, thirty, and fifty centimes a head, according
to location?

I. SCENES FROM THE LIFE OF MOSES
In Seven Tableaux
Beginning with the Bulrushes

II. THE SIOUX'S REVENGE
A Drama of Blood

III. THE SIGHTS OF PARIS
In Twelve Tableaux

In fact, the tent was already full, and the Toastmaster reluctantly turned up his coat-collar against the rain, and marched on. But what editorial instinct was revealed in that varied catalogue of dramatic delights! Many a time has the Toastmaster turned the leaves of certain back numbers of the Atlantic, especially remembered for their success or failure with the public, and tried to analyze the causes of their popularity or their neglect. Yet it may have been time wasted. Could the Ardennes people have told whether it was Moses, the Red Indian, or the Boulevard — or the combination of the three — that lured their centimes from their pockets? Neither can the present-day critic infallibly decide whether it was too many — or not enough — Bulrushes, too much or too little of the Sioux's Revenge, which made or marred the fortunes of those well-remembered issues of the Atlantic Monthly.

The one thing certain, among these accidents of short-lived glory and short-lived disappointment, these shiftings of scene and subject, and tactics altered from decade to decade, is that after all there is something in the Atlantic which does not change. From the beginning,

certain men have expressed in it unwaver-
ing ideals, an abiding vision of a better United
States of America. Some of these writers happily survive. Others, later-born, have instinctively aligned themselves with them. No one
who lingers over the rows of bound volumes
can fail to perceive, beneath the altering fashions of speech, an Atlantic "body of doctrine,"
— an interpretation, at once sound and fine,
of our American civilization. To this persistent
faith in the things that are excellent is due the
measure of permanence which the magazine has
won. "They pounded and we pounded," ex-
plained the simple-hearted Duke after Water-
loo, "but we pounded longest."

THE CENTENARY OF HAWTHORNE

The Centenary of Hawthorne[1]

In watching a performance of Shakespeare's most famous play, the attention of the spectator is arrested by one essentially solitary figure. Surrounded by the personages of a barbaric court, who eye him with curiosity, respect, or secret apprehension, stands a grave young man garbed in black. His bearing is princely. He begins to speak; but he veils deep ironic parables in a tone of perfect deference and courtesy. In vain do the king and queen utter their resonant commonplaces, and cast troubled glances at each other. They cannot sound him. How much does the prince know? What does he think? What will he do? He is inscrutable.

As the play runs its course, certain traits of

[1] An address delivered at Bowdoin College in commemoration of the one hundredth anniversary of Hawthorne's birth.

Hamlet become clear enough. He is of melancholy disposition, and of an intellectual cast of mind. He has "the courtier's, scholar's, soldier's, eye, tongue, sword." He has won the friendship of a man and the love of a woman. He possesses an exquisite humor, and delights in talk. He is reverent; believing in the powers of good, and fearing the powers of evil. He has a restless intelligence which probes into the secret places of human life. He broods over man's mortality, and plays with it imaginatively. He has infirmities of will, yet there is in him something dangerous, which on occasion sweeps all before him. For the space of some three hours we can observe this creation of Shakespeare play his part, — listening, planning, conversing, avenging, dying. Yet no one has ever plucked out the heart of his mystery. No actor or critic or lonely reader has ever been able to pronounce to us, indubitably and without fear of contradiction, what manner of man this Hamlet really is.

In the best-known and best-loved circle of our American writers there is likewise one figure who stands in a sort of involuntary isolation. Nathaniel Hawthorne had, indeed, warm and faithful friends. His affectionate family have

[66]

loved to dwell upon the details of his domestic life. He moved as an equal among a few of the best spirits of his time. The impression he made upon them may be traced in the journals of Longfellow and Emerson, the letters of Browning and Story and Lowell, the recollections of Bridge and Fields. His writings have been analyzed by accomplished critics. He was himself a diarist of extraordinary minuteness and precision, and, thanks to his own descriptions, we can still see him sitting with the tavern-haunters of North Adams, with the "defiant Democrats" in the Salem Custom House, with the blameless sea-captains in Mrs. Blodgett's boarding-house in Liverpool; we can stand by his side in the art-galleries of Florence and the studios of Rome. He died but forty years ago, and many living men and women remember him with strange vividness. Yet he remains, after all, a man apart. Mystery gathers about him, even while the annalists and the critics are striving to make his portrait clear.

Certain characteristics of Hawthorne are of course indisputable, and it is not fantastic to add that some of these qualities bear a curious resemblance to those of that very Prince of Denmark who seems more real to us than do most living men. Hawthorne was a gentleman; in body the mould of form, and graced with a noble mind. Like Hamlet, he loved to discourse with unlettered people, with wandering artists, with local humorists, although without ever losing his own dignity and inviolable reserve. He had irony for the pretentious, kindness for the simple-hearted, merciless wit for the fools. He liked to speculate about men and women, about temptation and sin and punishment; but he remained, like Hamlet, clear-sighted enough to distinguish between the thing in itself and the thing as it appeared to him in his solitude and melancholy. His closest friends, like Horatio Bridge and W. D. Ticknor, were men of marked justice and sanity of mind, — of the true Horatio type. Hawthorne was capable, if need be, of passionate and swift action, for all his gentleness and exquisite courtesy of demeanor. Toward the last he had, like Hamlet, his forebodings, — "such a kind of gain-giving, as would perhaps trouble a woman"; and he died, like Hamlet, in silence, conscious of an unfinished task.

We celebrate, in this summer time, the centenary of Hawthorne's birth. It is possible to understand him, in relation to his generation, better than he was understood in the middle of the nineteenth century, though we can scarcely praise him more generously than did those few contemporaries who, like Poe, made adequate recognition of his genius. If we cannot penetrate to the heart of his mystery, we can nevertheless perceive the nature of it. Critics will long continue to assess the precise value of his contributions to literature, and to assign his place in the development of his chosen art of romance-writing. But we who are gathered in his honor at the college of his choice may leave to the specialists the discussion of this and that detail of his craftsmanship. In a world where literary values, and the very basis of literary judgments, shift as they seem to be shifting in our contemporary civilization, it is impossible to predict what Hawthorne's popular rank will be in another hundred years. But we can at least say why two generations of Americans have respected Hawthorne's character and admired his writings. We can draw once more in memory the outward features of the man, and, before they fade again into the shadow, may assert our own faith in the enduring significance of his work.

No glimpse of Hawthorne, at any period of his career, is without charm; yet a peculiar fascination attaches to those pictures of the handsome, brooding, impenetrable boy which have been sketched, in lines all too few, by his college classmates. Here in a rustic school of learning, on the edge of the wilderness, our student found his Wittenberg. His contact with books had been that of the well-bred New England lad of a day when books were still respected. He had had free choice among them, and had read, before he was fourteen, Rousseau and the "Newgate Calendar," while the first book purchased with his own money was Spenser's "Faerie Queene." But under the Brunswick pines he was to find a better thing than books: namely, friendship. When Hawthorne matriculated in 1821, Bowdoin College had had but nineteen years of struggling life. There were a handful of professors and slightly more than a hundred students. Yet the place already had character, and it somehow bred aspiration. It is a suggestive coincidence, that in sketching Bowdoin College under an assumed name in his first book, "Fanshawe," Hawthorne pictures his academic hero as mastered by the "dream of undying fame"; and that

fifty years later, when his classmate Longfellow
described the college of his youth in the noble
" Morituri Salutamus," it was in the words, —

> Ye halls, in whose seclusion and repose
> Phantoms of fame, like exhalations, rose.

To many of those dreaming youths, fame, of
various degrees, became a reality. In Hawthorne's class were Longfellow, Cheever, Ab-
bott, and Cilley; among his college mates were
the highly honored names of Appleton, Bell,
Fessenden, Pierce, Stowe, Prentiss, Hale.
Among such ambitious companions, the shy
young Hawthorne held quietly to his own path.
He seems to have liked the plain, country-bred
lads better than the sons of wealth and social
opportunity; he belonged to the more demo-
cratic of the two literary societies. The scanty
records of his undergraduate life tell us something of him, although not much: he rooms in
Maine Hall, he boards at Mrs. Dunning's, he
is fined for card-playing, refuses to declaim,
writes better Latin and English prose than the
others, — but that is about all. One trait is,
indeed, marked, and it is a wholesome one:
namely, tenacity of friendship, — quite consist-
ent with a certain cool, obstinate independence.

Nearly forty years after graduation Hawthorne dedicated a book, "Our Old Home," to his college friend Franklin Pierce, who had become in 1863 extremely unpopular at the North. His publishers, with professional caution, advised Hawthorne not to ruin the chances of his book by dedicating it to the discredited ex-President. Whereupon Hawthorne wrote to them, in words that should be dear to all who believe in the vitality of college attachments : —

"I find that it would be a piece of poltroonery in me to withdraw either the dedication or the dedicatory letter. My long and intimate relations with Pierce render the dedication altogether proper, especially as regards this book, which would have had no existence without his kindness; and if he is so exceedingly unpopular that his name is enough to sink the volume, there is so much the more need that an old friend should stand by him. I cannot, merely on account of pecuniary profit or literary reputation, go back from what I have deliberately thought and felt it right to do; and if I were to tear out the dedication, I should never look at the volume again without remorse and shame."

Although the young Hawthorne came no

nearer winning academic distinction than Lowell or Thackeray, his college career betrays everywhere this steady insistence upon what he deliberately thought and felt it right to do. He had his own inner life, and if Bowdoin did not impart to him all the manifold intellectual and spiritual culture which an old-world university in theory possesses, he found there freedom, health, and a few men to love. One at least of these friends perceived the genius which was latent in the dark-haired, keen-eyed, rosy-cheeked boy, so reticent, so obstinate, so loyal. The clairvoyant was his classmate Bridge. In the preface to the "Snow Image" Hawthorne wrote, in sentences that every Bowdoin man perhaps knows by heart, yet so winning in their sentiment and phrase that they tempt quotation:—

"If anybody is responsible for my being at this day an author, it is yourself. I know not whence your faith came; but, while we were lads together at a country college,—gathering blueberries, in study-hours, under those tall academic vines; or watching the great logs, as they tumbled along the current of the Androscoggin; or shooting pigeons and gray squirrels in the woods; or bat-fowling in the summer twilight;

or catching trouts in that shadowy little stream
which, I suppose, is still wandering riverward
through the forest, — though you and I will
never cast a line in it again, — two idle lads, in
short, doing a hundred things that the Faculty
never heard of, or else it had been the worse
for us, — still, it was your prognostic of your
friend's destiny, that he was to be a writer of
fiction."

But what sort of writer of fiction? Many
elements contribute to the answer to that question. There are lines of literary inheritance to
be reckoned with; influences of race and nationality and epoch play their part. But of all
the factors that shaped Hawthorne's career as
a writer, Salem inevitably comes first. Back to
that weather-beaten, decrepit seaport Hawthorne returned when the bright college days
were over. The gray mist of the place settles
about him and gathers within him, and for a
dozen years one can scarcely tell whether he
is man or spectre. All that is certain is that
he is alone. His classmates fare forth eagerly
into law, politics, business. But Hawthorne
has no taste for any of the professions. He
lingers on in Salem, sharing the scanty income

of his mother and sisters, reading desultory
books, taking long nocturnal and daytime ram-
bles, brooding, dreaming, and trying to learn
in his dismal chamber to write stories about
human life.

Many years later he penned this pathetic
fragment of autobiography : —

"For a long, long while I have been occasionally visited with a singular dream; and I
have an impression that I have dreamed it ever
since I have been in England. It is, that I am
still at college, — or, sometimes, even at school,
— and there is a sense that I have been there
unconscionably long, and have quite failed to
make such progress as my contemporaries have
done; and I seem to meet some of them with
a feeling of shame and depression that broods
over me as I think of it, even when awake.
This dream, recurring all through these twenty
or thirty years, must be one of the effects of
that heavy seclusion in which I shut myself up
after leaving college, when everybody moved
onward and left me behind."

Such tragedies, unrelieved by any later victo-
ries of the spirit, are familiar enough to college
men. As the roll is called at their reunions,

[75]

there will always be here and there a name,
once rich in promise, of some man who has
"gone to seed." The sojourn of Hawthorne
in Salem is an old story now. Nothing new is
to be added to the record of morbid physical
isolation and of intellectual solitude. Set those
twelve years over against the corresponding
twelve in the life of Scott, Balzac, Dickens,
Turgénieff, and they have a ghostly pallor.
True, Hawthorne's separation from the world
preserved him from those distractions which
often dissipate the powers of the artist. He
kept, as he said, the dew of his youth and the
freshness of his heart. His unbroken leisure
left him free to ponder upon a few permanent
objects of meditation, and no one can say how
much his romances may not have gained thereby
in depth of tone and concentration of inten-
tion.

Yet the plain fact remains that he hated his
self-imposed prison, even while he lacked vigor
to escape from it. "There is no fate in the
world so horrible as to have no share in either
its joys or its sorrows"; thus he writes in 1837
to Longfellow, who had already made a career
and tasted deep of both sorrow and joy. And

Hawthorne's sombre seclusion was affecting his nascent art as well as his life. " I have another great difficulty," he adds to Longfellow, "in the lack of materials; for I have seen so little of the world that I have nothing but thin air to concoct my stories of." Strip the veil of romantic mystery from these Salem years, and they show their sinister significance. It was an abnormal, melancholy existence, which sapped Hawthorne's physical vitality and left its twilight upon his soul and upon the beautiful pages of his books.

The artistic record of that period is preserved in " Twice-Told Tales," a collection of some twoscore stories, none of which, on their first publication, had been signed with the author's name. Hawthorne said of them afterward, — and it is the final word of criticism as well as a confession of his way of life while composing them, — " They have the pale tint of flowers that blossomed in too retired a shade."

Nevertheless the flowers did blossom in spite of all. The soil would have been better had it been enriched and watered, yet it was Hawthorne's native soil. For two hundred years his ancestors had trodden the Salem streets; they had gone to sea, had persecuted the witches, had whipped Quaker women, had helped to build a commonwealth. He had no particular pride in them or love for them, but he could not escape the bond of kinship. Toward the more hospitable and cultivated aspects of Salem society in his own day,— the Salem of the Pickerings and Saltonstalls and Storys, — toward the dignity and beauty that still clothe the stately houses of Chestnut Street, Hawthorne remained indifferent. His imagination homed back to the superstition-burdened past, with its dark enthusiasms, its stern sense of law. Open the mouldering folio of Cotton Mather's "Magnalia" and you will discover the men and the scenes that haunted Hawthorne's mind as he sat in his dusky chamber writing tales.

He practiced himself also, with unwearied patience, in reporting the trivial incidents of the life around him, until he had developed a descriptive style marked by exceptional physical accuracy, and yet subtly suggestive, too. Listen to this lonely and as yet scarcely recognized man of letters, as he gives counsel in 1843 to his friend Horatio Bridge, who had also taken his pen in hand:—

[78]

"Begin to write always before the impression of novelty has worn off from your mind, else you will be apt to think that the peculiarities which at first attracted you are not worth recording; yet these slight peculiarities are the very things that make the most vivid impression upon the reader. Think nothing too trifling to set down, so it be in the smallest degree characteristic. You will be surprised to find on re-perusing your journal what an importance and graphic power these little particulars assume."

This is the assured tone of the finished craftsman. And he is careful to add: "I would advise you not to stick too accurately to the bare fact, either in your descriptions or your narrative; else your hand will be cramped and the result will be a want of freedom that will deprive you of a higher truth than that which you strive to attain."

Pale blossoms, indeed, are many of these earlier stories, yet genius was stirring at their root, and their growth was guided by a hand that already distinguished between the lower truth of fact and the higher truth of imagination. Sunshine was all that was needed, and

by and by, though tardily, the sunshine came.
Hawthorne falls in love; he craves and finds
contact with "the material world"; he goes to
work in the Boston Custom House; he makes
investment of money and coöperation at Brook
Farm, where his handsome figure and quizzical
smile seem almost substantial now, among the
ghosts of once eager reformers that flit about
that deserted hillside. He marries a charming
woman, and lives with her in the Old Manse
at Concord for four years of idyllic happiness.
He publishes a new collection of tales, marked
by originality of conception, a delicate sense of
form, and deep moral significance. He goes
picnicking with politicians, too, and gets appointed surveyor of the port of Salem. He is
doing a man's work in the world now, and in
spite of some humorous grumbling and the
neglect of his true calling, takes a manly satisfaction in it. But partisan politics rarely did
America a better service than in 1849, when
the Whig administration at Washington threw
Hawthorne out of office. He soon steadied
himself under the bitter blow, — writing to
George S. Hillard, "I have come to feel that
it is not good for me to be here. I am in a

lower moral state than I have been,—a duller intellectual one. So let me go; and under God's providence, I shall arrive at something better." His admirable wife was—womanlike—more concrete. When he told her that he had been superseded, she exclaimed, "Oh, then you can write your book!"

This book, as every one knows, was the "Scarlet Letter," that incomparable masterpiece of American fiction, which has long since taken its place among the great literature of the world. The boyish dream of Fame, analyzed in so many exquisite parables during his weary years of waiting, had at last come true for him. He was too unworldly to value it over-much, but he took a quiet pleasure in his success, without losing his cool, detached attitude toward his own creations. "Some parts of the 'Scarlet Letter,'" he pronounces, "are powerfully written." His long apprenticeship in one of the most exacting fields of literary composition was over. He was forty-six; and he had but fourteen more years to live. The first two of these were the most rich in production, for they brought forth the "House of the Seven Gables," that well-nigh faultless romance of Old

Salem; the beautiful "Wonder-Book," written in six weeks, with marvelous technical mastery of a difficult *genre* of literature; and, finally, the shrewd, ironical, surprisingly novel handling of his Brook Farm material, the "Blithedale Romance."

When Hawthorne accepted the Liverpool consulship in 1853, he was already, what he has ever since remained, the foremost of our fiction writers. His extended sojourn abroad illuminated his mind in many ways, but it can scarcely be said to have contributed new elements to his art. It brought him again into contact with executive duties, always scrupulously fulfilled; with new types of men and new scenes; and with a whole world of pictorial and plastic art, hitherto undreamed of. The record of it may be read in his laborious notebooks and in one profoundly imaginative romance. But Hawthorne's spiritual commerce with Europe came, on the whole, too late; both in England and Italy he remained the observant alien. One likes him none the less for a certain sturdy provinciality, — a touch even, here and there, of honest Philistinism. But one misses, in the records of these later years, the spontaneity, the vigor, the penetration, which marked the more fragmentary "American Note-Books." The unseen springs of vitality in him were beginning to fail; the shadows, dispersed by many a year of happiness, were beginning to close in once more. Longfellow notes in his diary, March 1, 1860: "A soft rain falling all day long, and all day long I read the 'Marble Faun.' A wonderful book; but with the old dull pain in it that runs through all of Hawthorne's writings."

It was in that year that the romancer returned home, and settled at the Wayside in Concord. War-time was nearing. Hawthorne, never an eager politician in any cause, was perplexed about his country, gloomy about himself. He wrote indeed, with his customary skill of surface composition, upon a new romance whose theme was the elixir of immortality. "I have a notion," he writes to Longfellow, "that the last book will be my best, and full of wisdom about matters of life and death." But it was fitful, despairing work, without unity of architecture. He sketched it now under one title, now under another. At last he prepared the opening chapter for the Atlantic Monthly,

but in May, 1864, the unfinished manuscript
rested upon his coffin. And so there passes
from sight our New England Hamlet, with his
grave beauty, his rich, mournful accents, his
half-told wisdom about matters of life and
death.

Yet not in these events of his outward career,
natural as it is to recall them now, but in the
peculiar processes of his creative activity, shall
we find, if at all, the secret of that power which
gives Hawthorne his unique position in our literature. First among those deep instincts which
give unity to his character and his books, should
be placed his choice of moral problems as material for his art. For nearly half a century we
have witnessed painstaking endeavors to base
the art of fiction upon the science of physiology.
Men of massive talent have wrought at such
books, but their experiments are already crum-
bling. And we have had schools of fiction dealing with the mere intellect, registering the subtle
influence of mind upon mind, and the open
struggle of mind with mind, or playing with extraordinary cleverness upon the surface of motives, while ignoring a whole world of profound
emotions. But the greatest masters of English

fiction have never forgotten that man has a conscience. The novelist who ignores the moral and
spiritual nature abandons the very field of fiction where the highest triumphs have been won.
There is a word to describe this field, — a word
broader than either " mind " or "conscience,"
and inclusive both of mental processes and spiritual perceptions. It is the word " heart."

In the " Blithedale Romance," Westervelt,
the embodiment of intellectual acuteness, is perplexed and irritated to find that Zenobia has
drowned herself. He cannot grasp her motive.
" Her mind was active and various in its powers," said he. " She had life's summer all before
her, and a hundred varieties of brilliant success.
How forcibly she might have wrought upon the
world! Every prize that could be worth a woman's having — and many prizes which other
women are too timid to desire — lay within Zenobia's reach." Then, in a note that Hawthorne
touches quietly, but unerringly, Miles Cover-
dale answers : " In all this, there would have
been nothing to satisfy her heart." Even the
romance-writer, according to Hawthorne's own
dictum, "sins unpardonably as far as he swerves
aside from the truth of the human heart."

To interpret that truth was his artistic task. He was haunted by moral problems. The extraordinary fragment, "Ethan Brand," is an attempt to solve the problem of the development of the intellect at the expense of the soul. In "Rappaccini's Daughter" the father's love of scientific experiment overmasters his love for his child. In the "Christmas Banquet" we have a man who misses the secret that gives substance to a world of shadows. The "Scarlet Letter" is a study of the workings of conscience after a committed crime; the "House of the Seven Gables" is devoted to the legacy of ancestral guilt and its mediation; the "Marble Faun" to the influence of a sin upon the development of character.

Why did Hawthorne's imagination fasten upon subjects like these? It is not enough to say that he wrote under the influence of Puritanism. Too much has been made, by his critics, of such phrases as "Puritan gloom" and "the morbid New England conscience." It is true that Hawthorne inherited from Puritan ancestors a certain tenseness of fibre, a sensitiveness of conscience, a conviction of the reality of the moral life. It is also true that he was in-

tensely interested in Puritanism as an historic
phenomenon. It gave him the material he
needed. How thoroughly he apprehended both
the spirit and the outward form of life in early
New England is evidenced by his " Legends of
the Province House," "Goodman Brown," the
"Gentle Boy," the " Minister's Black Veil."
Yet neither his inheritance in Puritanism nor his
profound study of it is enough to account satis-
factorily for his choice of themes for his stories.
Judged by his reading, by his friends and associations, by the spiritual emancipation which
was already liberalizing New England when he
began to write, he was Transcendentalist rather
than Puritan. Puritan theology, as such, had no
hold upon him personally; he was not even a
church-goer. One can only say that he was
drawn to moral problems by the natural gravi-
tation of his own mind, just as Newman was
inevitably attracted to theology, or Darwin to
science. From the days of Job to the day of
Ibsen and Maeterlinck there has been here and
there a person able to find in the moral nature
of man material for the creative imagination.
Hawthorne was one of these persons; he was
nurtured by Puritanism but not created by it.

A striking illustration of this habit of his mind is found in the introduction to his "Mosses from an Old Manse," where he repeats a story of the Concord fight, which had been told to him by Lowell. On that famous April morning, a youth who had been chopping wood for the Concord minister was drawn by curiosity to the battlefield, the axe still in his hand. He encountered a wounded British soldier, and in a nervous impulse of momentary terror dealt him a fatal blow. "The story," says Hawthorne, "comes home to me like truth. Oftentimes, as an intellectual and moral exercise, I have sought to follow that poor youth through his subsequent career, and observe how his soul was tortured by the blood stain, contracted as it had been before the long custom of war had robbed human life of its sanctity, and while it still seemed murderous to slay a brother man. That one circumstance has borne more fruit for me than all that history tells us of the fight." Observe that Hawthorne finds "an intellectual and moral exercise" in brooding over the question of the young man's responsibility. This may be called, if one pleases, the working of the morbid Puritan conscience. But it is also the very stuff out of which Greek tragedy is woven. It is the same brooding that is back of "Othello" and "Macbeth." "England is not the world," says an old courtier in one of Schiller's plays. New England has no monoply of the conscience.

The present generation has grown somewhat impatient of all analysis of that tragic guilt which our weak humanity may so easily incur. No doubt it is no very cheerful occupation. The anatomist of the heart develops a professional instinct for morbid pathology; he forsakes, perhaps too often, the normal organ for the abnormal. In his search for motives, it is easy for him to fall into casuistry; to impute guilt where there is none; to discover moral pitfalls where the ground is really smooth. It is with real satisfaction, with a positive glee, that Browning's monk in the "Spanish Cloister" cries, —

> "There's a great text in Galatians,
> Once you trip on it, entails
> Twenty-nine distinct damnations,
> One sure, if another fails."

Solitude is a prolific breeder of fancies like these. Over the windows of the romancer's lonely study, as of the monk's cell, the cobwebs may gather till the whole sky seems darkened. But there is other darkness, too, terribly real. "I do not see any sin in the world," said Hawthorne's brilliant contemporary, George Sand, "but I see a great deal of ignorance." Not so with his profounder insight. The presence of evil in the human heart, palpable, like that gross darkness which could be touched, was one of the axioms of his thinking. Without it, he would have been but a sacrilegious juggler.

The solitariness of Hawthorne's life, particularly in its formative years, united with a habit of ruminating over his work to determine in some measure the character of his themes. His note-books, which have never been adequately studied in their relation to his finished stories, are filled with random suggestions. But the purely fanciful themes were for the most part silently discarded ; those that really bore fruit are the imaginative ones. To this long brooding of a fertile mind over an apparently insignificant symbol we are indebted for the rarest productions of Hawthorne's genius. To take the most familiar example, it was in his tale of "Endicott and the Red Cross" that he first described "a young woman with no mean share of beauty, whose doom it was to wear the letter A, embroidered in scarlet cloth, on the breast of her gown." Miss Elizabeth Peabody said promptly, "We shall hear of that letter by and by";—and year after year that bit of embroidery glowed in the cloudy depths of Hawthorne's mind, until, when he drew it forth, it had become one of the master conceptions of the world's fiction. In similar fashion we can discover how the germs of the "House of the Seven Gables" and the "Marble Faun" were rooted, like vagrant truths, in the soil of that fertile imagination.

Yet a mind of this strange retentiveness — almost secretiveness — has, with all its fertility, certain defects. Some ideas committed to it become refined, over-refined, refined away. Symbolism, always a mode of art congenial to Hawthorne, is sometimes allowed to take the place of expression. The individual loses color and precision of outline, and becomes a mere type. Hawthorne's imagination seldom misled him; it had the inevitableness of genius. But his fancy, playing upon superficial resemblances, sporting with trivial objects, was his besetting weakness as a writer. It is none the less a weakness because it first drew public attention to him, or because it is in itself exquisite. Delicate and lovely as his fancies were, Hawthorne often played with them too long. He over-elaborated them; he painted his lily instead of letting it alone. It is true that as he advanced in life there is less and less of this. Contact with the world, with real joys and sorrows, deepened his insight, and dispelled some of the pretty, playful, soap-bubble allegories with which his more idle and solitary hours had been too often filled. He might have stayed in Salem and de-scribed Town Pumps and invented Celestial Railroads to the end of his days without draw-ing any nearer to the "Scarlet Letter." But little by little his powers were directed upon adequate objects; his imagination, rather than his fancy, dictated his choice of themes; and he followed that unerring guide.

Fortunate, also, was his instinct for shaping his work of art from that which lay nearest. All of his romances except one, and all of his short stories except a very few, are given a New Eng-land background. To the task of describing the landscape and people most familiar to him, Hawthorne brought an extraordinary veracity, and a hand made deft by years of unwearied exercise. Yet he is equally effective in dealing with the Pilgrims, or the stately days of the Massachusetts Province. He loves, in stories like the Seven Gables, to bring the past, gray with legendary mist, into the daylight of the present. Here the foreground and background are perfectly harmonized; the present is significant in proportion as its tones are mellowed and reinforced by the sombre past. Thus Hilda and Kenyon, New Englanders of Hawthorne's day, walk over the bloodstained pavements of old Rome, and the ghostly shadows of the Eternal City are about them as they move. Hawthorne himself considered the "House of the Seven Gables" and the "Marble Faun" his best achievements. They belong to the same type. Time and place and circumstance conformed to his feeling for the Romantic. Indeed, his sensitiveness to the Romantic note affects his characters throughout. They include a wide range of individualities, but they are not depicted by the usual methods of realistic portraiture. New Englanders in the main, few of them exhibit that New England eccentricity of speech and manner so assiduously observed by short-story writers since Hawthorne's time. He did not trouble himself — and us — with dialect. Indeed, all his characters, like Browning's, talk much the same language. His men and women are visible through a certain atmosphere which does not blur their features, yet softens them. Even his fullest and richest personalities, like Zenobia, maintain a distance from us.

His plots likewise, various as they are, have the simplicity of true Romance. His most widely read production, the story of Hester Prynne and Arthur Dimmesdale, has practically no plot whatever; it is a study of a situation. For moral problems, in spite of the ingenious practice of Mr. Henry James and Mr. Meredith, can usually be reduced to a very simple equation. An elaborate, many-threaded plot, full of incidents and surprises, of unexpected labyrinths and heaven-sent clues, would destroy the very atmosphere which Hawthorne seeks to create. The action of his romances is seldom dramatic, in the strict sense of the word. To dramatize the "Scarlet Letter" is to coarsen it. The deliberate action, the internal moral conflict, the subtle revelation of character, are all suited to the descriptive, not the dramaturgic method. They are in perfect keeping with the tone which Hawthorne instinctively maintained. He placed the persons who were to exemplify his themes now in the present, now in the past, if possible in the half-light of mingled past and present, and out of the simplest, most familiar materials he learned to compose a picture so perfect in detail, so harmonious in key, that even were the theme of slight significance, he would still vindicate his right to a high place among literary artists.

Yet perhaps the most convincing test of Hawthorne's merit is one of the most obvious. Open one of his books anywhere, and read a page aloud. Whatever else there may be, here is style. Hawthorne was once asked the secret of his style. He replied dryly that it was the result of a great deal of practice; that it came from the desire to tell the simple truth as honestly and vividly as he could. We may place alongside of this matter-of-fact confession a whimsical dream which he once noted in his journal, to the effect that the world had become dissatisfied with the inaccurate manner in which facts were reported, and had employed him at a salary of a thousand dollars a year, to relate things of importance exactly as they happened.

Is simple truth-telling, then, explanation
enough? Hawthorne had, indeed, a passion for
observing and reporting facts. Sometimes these
facts are insignificant. For instance: "The
aromatic odor of peat smoke in the sunny au-
tumnal air is very pleasant." Mr. Henry James
has remarked of this sentence that when a man
turned thirty gives a place in his mind — and
his inkstand — to such trifles as these, it is
because nothing else of superior importance
demands admission. But this is much like saying that because a botanist happens to put a
dandelion into his can he has, therefore, no eye
for an orchid. To the genuine collector there
are no trifles, and Hawthorne had at one time
the collector's passion. No French or Russian
realist had more of it. Certain pages of his note-
books and early sketches make one exclaim,
"Here is a man with the gifts of Balzac or Tol-
stoi! Why might he not have become a great
realistic writer, endowed as he was with this
thirst for the actual? He would so well earn
that thousand dollars a year!" But the facts,
as such, were not enough to hold Hawthorne
long; he pressed on beyond the fact to the
truth behind it. As he developed, he collected

certain facts to the neglect of others. He observed, but he also philosophized. If, therefore, the technique of his descriptive work often
reminds us of the great realists, the use he
makes of his talent as an observer and reporter
forbids us to group him with them. He was
born with too curious an interest in the unseen
world. However striking his technical gifts, he
wrote as a romancer, a creator.

And what a writer this provincial New Englander is ! We talk glibly nowadays about painting and writing with one's eye on the object.
Hawthorne could do this when he chose ; but
think of writing with your eye on the consciences
of Arthur Dimmesdale and Hester Prynne,
and never relaxing your gaze till the book is
done ! What concentration of vision ! What
exposing power ! Hawthorne's vocabulary is
not extraordinarily large ; — nothing like Balzac's or Meredith's ; but the words are chosen
like David's five smooth stones out of the
brook. The sentences move in perfect poise.
Their ease is perhaps a little self-conscious ; —
pains have been taken with their dressing, — it
is not the careless inevitable grace of Thackeray, — but it is a finished grace of their own.

It is a style exquisitely simple, except in those passages where Hawthorne's fancy gets the better of him, and leads him into forced humor, all the worse for its air of cultivated exuberance. Yet even when he sins against simplicity, he is always transparently clear. The certainty of word and phrase, the firmness of outline are marvelous, when we consider the airy nature of much of his material; he may be building cloud-castles, but it is in so pure a sky that the white battlements and towers stand out sharp-edged as marble.

Because Hawthorne gave his work such an elaborate finish, some readers are apt to forget its underlying strength. Our own day of naturalistic impressionism and correct historical costuming has invented a hundred sensational and clever ways of tearing a passion to tatters. But it is well for us to remember that the real strength of a work of fiction is in the conception underlying it, and that the deepest currents of thought and feeling are

Too full for sound and foam.

Strong-fibred, sane, self-controlled, as was Hawthorne, one may nevertheless detect in his style that melancholy vibration which marks

the words of all—or almost all—those who
have interpreted through literature the more
mysterious aspects of life. This pathos is profound, though it is quiet; it is an undertone, but
not the fundamental tone; "the gloom and terror may lie deep, but deeper still is this eternal
beauty."

Yet the most marked quality of Hawthorne's
style is neither simplicity, nor clearness, nor reserve of strength, nor undertone of pathos. It
is rather its unbroken melody, its verbal rich-
ness. Its echoes linger in the ear; they wake old
echoes in the brain. The touch of a few other
men may be as perfect, the notes they evoke
more brilliant, certainly more gay; but Hawthorne's deep-toned instrument yields harmo-
nies inimitable and unforgettable. The critics
who talk of the colorless life of New England
and its colorless reflection in literature had
better open their Hawthorne once more. His
pages are steeped in color. They have a dusky
glory like the great window in Keats's "Eve of
St. Agnes":—

> . . . diamonded with panes of quaint device,
> Innumerable of stains and splendid dyes,
> As are the tiger-moth's deep-damask'd wings;

And in the midst, 'mong thousand heraldries,
And twilight saints, and dim emblazonings,
A shielded scutcheon blush'd with blood of queens and kings.

This subdued splendor of Hawthorne's coloring is a part of the very texture of his style; compared with it the brushwork of his successors seems thin and washy, or else crude and hard; it is like comparing a rug woven in Bokhara with one manufactured in Connecticut. But surely our New England soil is not wholly barren if even for once it has flowered into such a consummate artist as Nathaniel Hawthorne, who, while he devoted his art to the interpretation of truth, was nevertheless dowered with such instinct for beauty that his very words glow like gems and echo like music, and grant him a place among the few masters of English style.

After all, we do not celebrate the centenary of Hawthorne's birth merely because he was a skillful, an admirable writer. Rather do we take a solemn pride in commemorating one who steadfastly asserted the claims of spiritual things. He wrote in a generation fortunate in its balance between the hard material struggles of the colonist and pioneer, and the far more dangerous materialism that comes with luxury and power. America had lived through sufficient history to give perspective to her romancers; she had not yet undergone the demoralizing strain of prosperity which has followed upon the epoch of the Civil War. Never were Americans so profoundly idealistic, so temperamentally fit to understand the spiritualized art of Hawthorne, as between 1840 and 1860. And our pride in him is touched with a subtle regret at the disappearance of a fine civilization, provincial as it was. A more splendid civilization is still to come, no doubt; but the specific conditions that blossomed into many of Hawthorne's tales are irrevocably gone. Great as he seems when we look back, he seems still greater when we look around us. It is no service to Hawthorne's memory to disparage the industrious men and women who are producing our fiction of to-day. But to glance at them, and then to think of him, is to perceive the startling difference between talent and genius.

No one would claim that that genius was faultless in all its divinations. Feeble drawing, ineffective symbolism, morbid dallying with mortuary fancies, may indeed be detected in his books. That sound critic Edwin P. Whipple, who is passing into such ill-deserved oblivion, once said of Hawthorne: "He had spiritual insight, but it did not penetrate to the sources of spiritual joy." The note of robust triumph, of unquestioning faith in individual happiness and in the sure advance of human society, is indeed too rarely heard in his writings. In repeating his paternoster, the stress falls upon "Forgive us our trespasses" rather than upon "Thy Kingdom come."

Yet he believed that the sin and sorrow of humanity, inexplicable as they are, are not to be thought of as if we were apart from God. A neighbor of Hawthorne in Concord has recently written me that once, when death entered a household there, Hawthorne picked the finest sunflower from his garden, and sent it to the mourners by Mrs. Hawthorne with this message : "Tell them that the sunflower is a symbol of the sun, and that the sun is a symbol of the glory of God." A shy, simple act of neighborhood kindness,—yet treasured in one memory for more than forty years; and how much of Hawthorne there is in it! The quaint flower from an old-fashioned garden; the delicate sympathy; the perfect phrase; the faith in the power of a symbol to turn the perplexed soul to God! Hawthorne was no natural lover of darkness, but rather one who yearned for light. The gloom which haunts many of his pages is the long shadow cast by our mortal destiny upon a sensitive soul, conscious of kinship with the erring race of men. The mystery is our mystery, perceived, and not created, by that finely endowed mind and heart. The shadow is our shadow; the gleams of insight, the soft radiance of truth and beauty, are his own.

THE CENTENARY OF LONGFELLOW

The Centenary of Longfellow

WE allow the centenaries of our men of letters to pass without general observance. The one hundredth anniversaries of the births of Hawthorne and of Emerson were, indeed, duly celebrated at Brunswick, Salem, Concord, and Boston. But these were exercises of local piety, the expression of a laudable provincial pride. A wide national recognition of such anniversaries does not yet come easily to us; "they order this matter better in France," with a more spontaneous clashing of the cymbals, a more graceful processional to the shrine. It is possible that the anniversary of Longfellow's birth may be more generally and tenderly remembered than that of other American authors of his time. Multitudes of his countrymen, to whom Hawthorne and Poe were mere necromancers, and Emerson

a shining seraph announcing unintelligible
things, thought of Longfellow as a familiar
friend. But twenty-five years have already
elapsed since his death. To a busy republic,
swift to forget even its best servants, a quarter
of a century is a long period, and the startling
political and social changes which have been
brought about within that interval make it seem
even longer still. Longfellow's noble life and
work have indeed kept him in remembrance;
but apparently it is only Lincoln, among all
the figures of that generation, who has grown
steadily in popular fame.

It is inevitable that there should be some
reaction against the extraordinary popularity
which Longfellow's poetry enjoyed during his
lifetime. Nor should his most loyal admirers
quarrel with the spirit which to-day seeks to
scrutinize the causes of such a popularity. To
the true lover of books, the quality of a poet is
everything; the counting of the heads of the
poet's audience is but an idle occupation. It is
difficult for Colonel Higginson to write other-
wise than delightfully, but I wish that he had
not begun his " Life of Longfellow " by giving
the British Museum statistics of the demand for

Longfellow's writings, and the editions in the various languages of the world. Do not even the publicans and the historical novelists the same? Such figures — unless they cover more than a single generation — raise more doubts than they allay. Nowhere is a little wise distrust of the popular judgment more sanative than in the field of poetry. The literary mass-meeting settles nothing. If it records an enormous majority for some candidate to-day, it is likely to-morrow to vote his name wearisomely familiar, imitating that illogical but very human and likable Athenian who petulantly marked his ballot against Aristides.

Yet if a little skepticism as to the wisdom of the general contemporary verdict is wholesome, a complete skepticism is rash. I know a shrewd and slightly cynical publisher who insists that the popularity of a piece of literature is always in an inverse ratio to its excellence. This is a pleasing and easily remembered formula. It collapses, however, when you say " Hamlet." And I think it collapses when you say " Evangeline." The presumption may be, and for certain fastidious minds it always will be, that a popular poem cannot have a high literary rating.

But it is one of the most unsafe presumptions
upon which a critic can put out to sea. There is,
to be sure, a natural commonplaceness which
forms a solidarity of sympathy between certain
authors and their public. I once asked a poet:
" How does our friend Blank, the novelist, manage to hit the average vulgar taste with such wonderful accuracy ? " " He does n't *hit* it," said
the poet gloomily, " he *is* it." But this complete
identity of author and audience must be sharply
distinguished from that exquisite gift possessed
by a few men of essential distinction, — like
Gray, like Goethe, like Longfellow, — of giving
perfect expression to certain feelings which are

in widest commonalty spread.

Both of these classes of writers may produce a
widely popular poem or book. But the difference in the result is that which separates " David
Harum " from " The Vicar of Wakefield," and
"The Old Oaken Bucket" from the " Elegy in
a Country Churchyard." Longfellow, it is true,
sometimes allowed himself to print commonplace pieces. Like most poets, and like every
American poet of his generation except Poe, he
published too much. He had a sympathic per-

ception of the moods of unsophisticated people,
and he usually preferred to interpret such feelings rather than the more recondite aspects of
human experience. He felt, as we all feel, that
the rain is beautiful, and he did not hesitate to
say in verse, —

How beautiful is the rain !

That he ran a certain risk in thus carrying simplicity to the verge of guilelessness he must
have been aware, through the early and constant
parodies upon this vein of his poetry. But he
knew his course. He gained and held his great
circle of readers by precisely this obedience to
his instinct. His contemporaries felt what Emerson (with perhaps a touch of unconscious
patronage) wrote about "Hiawatha": " I have
always one foremost satisfaction in reading your
books, that I am safe." To speak safely to one
generation is to speak with some hazard to the
generations following, and Longfellow's beautiful work has already paid a penalty for his
overwhelming immediate success.

In one other respect, too, we must note a
sort of whispered reservation that is sometimes
made when Longfellow's name is spoken. One
need not fear to utter it, even in the magazine

to which he was such a friendly and honored contributor. Was he, after all, a great poet? Mr. Longfellow himself, with his delicate sense of literary values, would have respected the scruple which prompts such a question. One may easily imagine what he would have replied. He was once showing the Craigie House, with his unmatched courtesy, to one of those ignorant bores whom he patiently allowed to ravage his golden hours. The stranger asked if Shakespeare did not live somewhere about there. " I told him," said Mr. Longfellow, " I knew no such person in this neighborhood." Exactly. No such person as Shakespeare has ever been in the Cambridge Directory. But what of it? Why should size be snatched at as the chief criterion of poetic performance? The nightingale, type and symbol of all poets, is but a small brown bird.

How Longfellow himself regarded an indubitably great poet may be seen in his incomparable sonnets upon the " Divina Commedia." Dante's poem is there likened to a cathedral, within whose doors the tumult of the time dies away, —

> While the eternal ages watch and wait.

Old agonies and exultations haunt these shadows; here are echoes of tragedies and of celestial
voices. The windows are ablaze with saints and
martyrs; the organ sounds; the unseen choirs
sing the Latin hymns; and the head is bowed in
the presence of the ineffable mysteries of the
Faith. Nothing built by human hands has the
dark grandeur of such a minster. There is only
one other place that may be as sacred, — and
that is the home. To open Dante is like passing
within the solemn portal of a cathedral; to read
Longfellow is like entering the Craigie House.
The fine dignity of the vanished eighteenth
century is here. From the doorway stretches a
gentle landscape, with its winding river and low
hills. All around there is quiet beauty, with
lilacs and elms and green lawns sweet with children's voices; within the old mansion wait hospitality, and gracious courtesy, and the savor of
worn books, and the sanctities of long, intimate
converse with all lovely and honorable things.
It is a friend's roof, and it welcomes us in hours
when the cathedral oppresses or appalls.

It is no wonder that men and women of New
England blood are loyal to Longfellow. His

stock was of the finest of our sifted wheat. John
Alden, the young lover in his most perfect narrative poem,—that "bunch of May-flowers
from the Plymouth woods,"—was his maternal
ancestor. Among his forbears were men distinguished for gallantry in the country's service,
and for stainless integrity of private character.
His boyhood in Portland was typical of the
time and section, in its moral sweetness, its intellectual hunger and fine ambition. He had the
look of his family,—the slim straight figure,
the waving brown hair, the blue eyes, the quickly
flushed cheeks. He read in his father's library
the sound English classics of the eighteenth
century, but the first book to fascinate his imagination was Irving's "Sketch-Book." "I was
a schoolboy when it was published," he wrote
forty years afterward, "and read each succeed-
ing number with ever increasing wonder and
delight, spell-bound by its pleasant humor, its
melancholy tenderness, its atmosphere of re-
very,—nay, even by its gray-brown covers,
the shaded letters of its titles, and the fair, clear
type, which seemed an outward symbol of its
style." Such was the boy of whom—at the ripe
age of six—his schoolmaster had testified that

"his conduct last quarter was very correct and amiable," and of whom a classmate at Bowdoin — in that famous class of 1825 — said, "It appeared easy for him to avoid the unworthy."

One is reminded of the remark made by Puvis de Chavannes in the hour of his long-deferred triumph as an artist. "Who was your master?" he was asked. "I never had any master," said the painter, thinking perhaps of his restless, friendless journeys from one atelier to another; "my master has been a horror of certain things." That fineness of nature which made it seem easy for Longfellow, as for his classmate Hawthorne, to avoid the unworthy, was perfected by the firm intellectual discipline and the clear flame of aspiration that characterized the years spent in the struggling country college. Typical of that period was his unashamed acknowledgment of his heart's ambition, revealed in a well-known letter to his father: "The fact is, I most eagerly aspire after future eminence in literature; my whole soul burns most ardently for it, and every earthly thought centres in it." How charming it is, this boyish ardor! Longfellow's was but one of hundreds of such voices rising from every home of learning in New England, three quarters of a century ago. We hear them still, in the fresh tones of this eager, generous, high-minded youth, who had the good fortune to realize his dream.

It was fulfilled, as most dreams are, in unforeseen ways. Through the range and the quality of Longfellow's life-work he was enabled to perform a spiritual service for his countrymen. He was to become a national, rather than a merely provincial figure. In our imaginations, indeed, he lingers as a lovely flowering of all that was most fair in the New England temperament and training, in that long blossoming season which began with Emerson's "Nature" and ended—no one knows just when or how —within a decade or two after the close of the Civil War. There is but too much truth in Mr. Oliver Herford's witty description of the present-day New England as the abandoned farm of literature. Apparently the soil must lie fallow for a while, or some one must plough deeper than our melancholy short-story writers seem to go. But when the old orchard was bearing, what bloom and fruitage were hers!

Yet Longfellow was far more than a melo-

dious voice of that New England springtime.
It became his privilege to interpret to his generation the hitherto alien treasures of European
culture. He brought Spain and Italy, France
and Germany and the shadowy northern races,
into the consciousness of his countrymen.
While Irving and Bryant were the pioneers in
this adventure, it was through Longfellow,
more than any other man, that the poetry of
the Old World — the romance of town and
tower and storied stream, the figures of monk
and saint and man-at-arms, of troubadour and
minnesinger, of artist and builder and dreamer
—became the familiar possession of the New.

This immense service was made possible
through Longfellow's scholarship. When he
was graduated from Bowdoin, at the age of
eighteen, he had a good knowledge of Latin and
Greek, and a fair amount of French. Receiving
the promise of a professorship of modern languages at his alma mater, upon the condition
that he should prepare himself by European
study, he sailed in 1826 for a three years' ab-
sence. After two years and a half he was able
to write to his father: "I know you cannot be
dissatisfied with the progress I have made in

my studies. I speak honestly, not boastfully.
With the French and Spanish languages I am
familiarly conversant, so as to speak them cor-
rectly, and write them with as much ease and
fluency as I do the English. The Portuguese I
read without difficulty. And with regard to my
proficiency in the Italian, I have only to say
that all at the hotel where I lodge took me for
an Italian until I told them I was an American." He then proceeded to master German,
and in subsequent years familiarized himself
with several other languages of northern
Europe. During the five or six years of his
Bowdoin professorship, and for eighteen years
at Harvard, he gave careful and competent instruction in these languages, lecturing regularly
upon various foreign literatures, and superin-
tending the work of the picturesque and often
extremely difficult foreign gentlemen (the
"four-in-hand of outlandish animals all pulling the wrong way, except one") who acted as
his assistants. Of the extent and accuracy of
his linguistic attainments his published trans-
lations from no less than nine languages are a
sufficient proof. His college tasks left him
scanty leisure, his eyesight was early impaired,

and he gave himself freely to the claims of hospitality; and yet in spite of these drawbacks his acquaintance with the literatures of mediæval and modern Europe became extraordinary. He made no pretense, however, to strictly philological erudition, and he would probably have regarded with mild surprise the formidable apparatus of learning which our contemporary scholars love to bring to bear upon the weakest points in their opponent's line. One may even venture to think that Longfellow would have found such philological contests rather dull. He played by preference the open game, moving with a delightful swiftness and ease from folklore and drinking-song to missal and codex. His prose volumes, "Hyperion" and "Outre-Mer," reflect something of the variety of his reading, and his natural sympathy with that European Romantic movement which was still occupied, in the thirties, with revivifying the past and lending an emotional coloring to the present. For years after his return from his first long sojourn in Europe this seemed to be his calling: to give a few American boys some bright glimpses of those illuminated pages which had fascinated his own fancy.

Then, after a decade of teaching, came the revelation of his true power. He discovered that he was himself a poet. He had written boyish verses, such as we all write, and the constant practice in metrical translation had perfected his sense of poetical form. But here was a new impulse. His Journal notes [Dec. 6, 1838]: "A beautiful holy morning within me. I was softly excited, I knew not why; and wrote with peace in my heart and not without tears in my eyes, 'The Reaper and the Flowers, a Psalm of Death.' I have had an idea of this kind in my mind for a long time, without finding any expression for it in words. This morning it seemed to crystallize at once, without any effort of my own." How familiar that "soft excitement" is to those who listen to the confidences of the poets; and how inadequate an explanation, after all, of the miracle by which a poem comes into being!

Longfellow was now in his thirties. He had been called from Brunswick to Cambridge. The wife of his youth was dead in a foreign land, and he had returned from that melancholy second visit to Europe, to live with books and a few friends. His youthful ambition for eminence had deepened into a love of the beautiful and a desire to speak truth. "Fame must be looked upon only as an accessory," he wrote, in a heart-searching letter to his friend Greene. "If it has ever been a principal object with me — which I doubt — it is so no more." Like Hawthorne, he found fame when he ceased to seek it. "The Psalm of Life," "The Reaper and the Flowers," "The Wreck of the Hesperus," "The Skeleton in Armor," "The Rainy Day," "Maidenhood," "Excelsior," followed one another as thrushes follow one another in the deep woods at dawn, with melodies effortless and pure. Everybody listened. Two of these poems, "The Psalm of Life" and "Excelsior," have indeed paid the price of a too apt adjustment to the ethical mood of that "earnest" moment in America. They were not so much poems as calls to action, and now that two generations have passed, those trumpets rust upon the wall. It is enough that they had their glorious hour.

To appeal through verse to the national as well as to the individual conscience was not for Longfellow, as it was for Whittier and Lowell, a natural instinct. His path lay for the most

part outside the field of political poetry. Yet
by his anti-slavery poems of 1842 he placed
himself unmistakably on record against the
most gigantic evil of his day; and in his anti-
militaristic poem, "The Arsenal at Springfield,"
he protested against the most widespread evil
of our own. History loves to be ironical. Longfellow lived to see those very Springfield rifles
help to end slavery in the United States; he
lived to see "Enceladus arise" and shake off
by force of arms the shackles of Italy; but he
did not live long enough to hear his "holy
melodies" of international love succeed to the
diapasons of war. The high priests of the present
dispensation assure us that his vision of univer-
sal disarmament is only a dream, and a dangerous dream. Yet there are and will be others to
dream it until they make the dream come true.

The happiness of an assured recognition by
the public was now followed by the deeper joy
of a new home, but his habitation still remained
the Craigie House. Friends multiplied, although a chosen few, like Felton and Sumner,
had still their privileged place. Longfellow began to build in fancy a great poem, dealing with
no less vast a theme than "the various aspects

of Christendom in the Apostolic, Middle and Modern Ages." For thirty years it was to occupy his mind. The second portion, "The Golden Legend," was finished first: a lovely, full-blown rose of learning, of sympathetic insight, of imagination. The third part, "The New England Tragedies," followed after nearly a score of years; and "The Divine Tragedy," which now introduces the completed poem, was written last. Thus the poet's task was ultimately finished; whether it was truly accomplished, according to the measure of his aspiration, who can say? He was not by nature a tragic poet. The New England dramas, faithfully as they reproduce the colonial atmosphere, seem but a provincial conclusion for the poet's comprehensive scheme. The sacred theme of "The Divine Tragedy," and the scrupulous fidelity with which Longfellow weaves the words of the Scripture into his pattern, tend to remove the poem from the unimpeded scrutiny of criticism. We know that it possessed a deep significance to the author, that more is meant than meets the ear, completely as the ear is charmed. It is one of the instances, not rare in the history of letters, where a poet's greatest work — as conceived by himself — has been relatively unregarded by his public.

For it is unquestionable that to his contemporaries, both here and abroad, Longfellow was recognized as the author of tender lyrics, and of " Evangeline," " Hiawatha," and " The Courtship of Miles Standish." These narrative poems have become so secure a national possession that criticism seems an intrusion: it is like carrying a rifle into a national park. And it is to be suspected that the most formidably armed critic would return from his unlawful excursion with a rather empty bag. He would discover, no doubt, a few weak hexameters in " Evangeline," an occasional thinness of tone in " Hiawatha." He would point out the essentially bookish origin of all three poems, or in other words — what is true enough — that Longfellow loved to enter the House of Life by the library door. Very possibly there might never have been an " Evangeline " if there had not been a " Hermann and Dorothea " first. Very probably Felton and T. W. Parsons and other scholarly friends of Longfellow were right in their feeling that the dactylic measure of " Evangeline " is less suited to our

English speech-rhythms than the iambic. Certainly the hexameters of " Miles Standish," with their frequent iambic substitutions, are more supple and racy than those of the earlier poem. But this does not take us very far. We are no nearer the heart of the mystery of poetry for knowing that the rhythm of " Hiawatha " was borrowed from the Finnish "Kalevala," and that the legends were taken, with due acknowledgments, from Schoolcraft. After all, the crucial question about Hiawatha's canoe was not where he got his materials, but whether the finished craft would float ; and it is enough to say of the poem, as of the gayly colored canoe itself, —

> And the forest's life was in it,
> All its mystery and its magic,
> All the lightness of the birch-tree,
> All the toughness of the cedar,
> All the larch's supple sinews;
> And it floated on the river,
> Like a yellow leaf in Autumn,
> Like a yellow water-lily.

" Evangeline " had been finished on the poet's fortieth birthday, and "The Courtship of Miles Standish" was written when he was fifty-one. That decade, so rich in poetic pro-

ductiveness, was the happiest of Longfellow's
life. He had been granted what Southey, another library poet, had craved for himself, —

Books, children, leisure, all the heart desires.

Success — a ghastly calamity for some writers
— did not spoil the simplicity of his nature
and the sincerity of his art. As the years went
by, he discovered that college teaching, which
had been pleasant enough at first, grew weari-
some. His journal is full of half-humorous,
half-plaintive references to the "treadmill" and
the "yoke"; he likens himself to a miller, his
hair white with meal, trying to sing amid the
din and clatter; he finds it hard to lecture on
so delicate a subject as Petrarch "in this harsh
climate, in a college lecture-room, by broad
daylight." In 1854 he surrendered his college
chair to Lowell, and gave himself henceforward wholly to his true vocation. He could not,
indeed, summon the ungracious courage to
protect himself from the merciless demands of
callers, correspondents, and admirers of every
sort. In one week he wrote nothing but letters; in one forenoon he entertained fourteen
callers, thirteen of them English. But aside

from these intrusions, which are the unavoidable impost-tax upon popularity, he was enabled, in almost as full a degree as Tennyson after 1850, to ripen upon the sunny side of the wall. The sheltered life was best, no doubt, for that delicate nature of his, disliking to strive and cry in the streets, and finding, as he confesses in his journal, "life and its ways and ends prosaic in this country to the last degree." He was too true a poet not to feel the possibility of a poetic inspiration in the dominant chords of that competitive civilization which was already vibrating all about him. He notes in a morning walk: "I see the red dawn encircling the horizon, and hear the thundering railway trains, radiating in various directions from the city along their sounding bars, like the bass of some great anthem,—our national anthem." But he never —save possibly in "The Building of the Ship" —tried to set that anthem to music of his own. One is reminded of that other sensitive and withdrawn person, Nathaniel Hawthorne, who said regretfully of the rude life which he witnessed upon the wharves of Boston, "A better book than I shall ever write was there." Yet it would not be strange if both Hawthorne and Long-

fellow were to outlast the author of "McAn-
drew's Hymn."

In fact, the last decade—which has ordered
its writers to serve up life in the raw, to write
with their eye upon the object, and to sacrifice
beauty to the thrilling sense of contact with actual experience—has been hardly fair to the
Cambridge and Concord men. It is undeniable
that there was a transient phase of "softness" in
the forties, which Longfellow did not escape.
He thought it "exquisite to read good novels
in bed with waxlights in silver candlesticks,"
and exclaimed, after reading Frémont's account
of the Rocky Mountain expedition of 1842,
"But, ah, the discomforts!" He remained in
lifelong unacquaintance with the physical aspects of his own country. Yet we forget how
quickly the bookish man, provided he have the
searchlight of imagination upon his desk, can
dispense with first-hand observation of scenery.
Coleridge wrote the "Hymn to Mont Blanc"
and "The Ancient Mariner" without having seen the Vale of Chamonix and the tropic
ocean. The northwestern and southwestern
American landscapes in "Hiawatha" and
"Evangeline" are no less "true to nature" than

the realistic picture of the rainy morning in Sud-
bury, in the "Tales of a Wayside Inn." The
misfortune of the home-keeping poets lies not
so much in any artistic limitation, as in our own
lurking sense that some bolder and more en-
franchising spiritual adventures might have
been theirs if they had more often gone down
to the sea in ships and done business in great
waters.

Yet we know but little, either from his journal or his poems, of Longfellow's inner life.
When his hour of dreadful trial came, in 1861,
he met it with a gentleman's silent courage. In
the years that followed he turned again for solace
to his translation of Dante, begun long before.
He found also, in his device of the Wayside
Inn, a happy mode of linking together many a
mellow story which he still wished to tell. The
various Interludes reveal, to a fuller degree
than any previous work of his, the ease of the
finished artist, playful and adroit. The stories
are for the most part Old World tales, — of
Arabia and the East, of Sicily and Tuscany,
of the green Alsatian hills and the gray Baltic,
— but here too are "Paul Revere's Ride" and
"Lady Wentworth." It is inevitable that in

such a rich collection there should be some tales
in which Longfellow's masters in the story-tell-
ing art would have surpassed him; stories to
which Boccaccio would have imparted a gayer
drollery, or Chaucer a more robust breath of the
highroad. But we who have loved these stories
in youth rarely tire of them, and the most brilliant, I think, are those that are most completely
the product of Longfellow's own fancy, —

> — an invention of the Jew,
> Spun from the cobwebs of his brain,
> And of the same bright scarlet thread
> As was the Tale of Kambalu.

With the completion of "The Divine Tragedy," the trilogy now published under the title
"Christus: A Mystery" was finished. Longfellow began almost immediately another long
dramatic poem, "Michael Angelo," which was
found in his desk after his death. It is difficult
to characterize it fitly, or to realize all the subtle
bonds of affinity which drew the thoughts of
the aging Longfellow to the last survivor of the
greatest artistic period of Italy. Mr. Horace
Scudder, one of the most sympathetic and best-
equipped critics of American verse, used to consider this poem as Longfellow's *apologia pro*

vita sua, wherein the reader is always aware of
Longfellow's presence, "wise, calm, reflective,
musing over the large thoughts of life and art."
I confess that I cannot see so clearly as this
beneath the smooth, shadowed surface of the
poem. It is Longfellow's most finished blank
verse,—a verse that sings, mourns, and aspires,
but never quite laughs; indeed, this was no time
for laughter, after the sack of Rome. In lieu of
action, there is a succession of charming or grave
conversations, woven together out of the gos-
sipy pages of Cellini, Vasari, and many another
chronicler; to read them is to see again the yellowing travertine, the broken arches, and the
stone pines against the Roman sky; it is to feel
the pathos of unfulfilled dreams, of a titanic,
unavailing struggle against a petty world; in a
word, it is to watch the red melancholy sunset
of the Renaissance. But it is a strange *apologia*
for the American poet.

Although the last two decades of Longfellow's life produced these longer poems, with a
deeper symbolism which may escape the casual
reader, they also gave to the world some of his
best-known and most characteristic work. The
range of his poetic faculty and the ripeness of

his technical skill were exhibited in lyrics fully
as lovely and varied as the old: in descriptive
pieces like "Keramos" and "The Hanging of
the Crane"; in such personal and "occasional"
verses as "The Herons of Elmwood" and the
noble "Morituri Salutamus"; and finally in
sonnets,—like those upon Chaucer, Milton,
the "Divina Commedia," "A Nameless Grave,"
Felton, Sumner, "Nature," "My Books,"—
which are already secure among the imperish-
able treasures of the English language.

There is no formula which adequately ex-
plains and comments upon such a career. It is
apparent that Longfellow possessed, to a very
notable degree, an instinctive literary tact. He
knew, by a gift of nature, how to comport himself with moods and words, with forms of prose
and verse, with the traditions, conventions, unspoken wishes of his readers. Literary tact, like
social tact, is more easy to feel than to define. It
does not depend upon learning, for professional
scholars conspicuously lack it. Nor does it turn
upon mental power, or moral quality. Poe, who
could not live among men without making enemies, moved in and out of the borderland of
prose and verse with the inerrant grace of a wild

creature, sure-footed and quick-eyed. Lowell, whose social tact could be so perfect, sometimes allowed himself, out of sheer exuberance of spirits, to play a boyish leap-frog with the literary proprieties. The beautiful genius of Emerson often stood tongue-tied and awkward, confusing and confused, before problems of literary behavior which to the facile talent of Dr. Holmes were as simple as talking across a dinner-table. But Longfellow's literary tact was always impeccable: he divined what could and could not be said and done under the circumstances; he escorted the Muses to the banquet hall without stepping on their robes; he met the unspoken thought with the desired word, and — a greater gift than this — he knew when to be silent.

It is possible to misjudge this fineness of artistic instinct, this professional dexterity. Browning, who analyzed, and perhaps over-analyzed, Andrea del Sarto as the "faultless painter," has, by dint of forcing us to consider what Andrea lacked, made us too forgetful of what he really possessed. Once made aware of the Florentine's limitations in passion and imagination, we tend, under the spell of Browning's genius, to give him insufficient credit even for

his grace in composition, his pleasant coloring,
his suave facility. And it is true that the greatest
painters have something which Andrea somehow missed. No doubt the most masterful poets
have certain qualities which we do not find in
Longfellow. But that is no reason for failing to
recognize the qualities which he did command
in well-nigh flawless perfection. There are can-
did readers, unquestionably, who feel that they
have outgrown him. But for one, I can never
hear such a confession without a sort of pain. It
may be that these readers are naturally passing
on from room to room of the endless palace of
poetry. It may be that they seek a ruder, more
athletic exercise of the mind than Longfellow
offers them, and that they find this stimulus in
Browning or Whitman or Lucretius. Concerning such instinctive preferences there can be no
debate; the world of letters is fortunately very
wide. But sometimes, it is to be feared, a loss
of enjoyment in Longfellow is the symbol of a
lessening love for what is simple, graceful, and
refined.

These characteristics of Longfellow's art
were rooted in his nature. Here is an entry
from his journal, on August 4, 1836: "A day

[134]

of quiet and true enjoyment, travelling from Thun to Entlebuch on our way to Lucerne. The time glided too swiftly away. We read the 'Genevieve' of Coleridge and the 'Christabel' and many scraps of song, and little German ballads of Uhland, simple and strange. At noon we stopped at Langnau, and walked into the fields, and sat down by a stream of pure water that turned a mill; and a little girl came out of the mill and brought us cherries; and the shadow of the trees was pleasant, and my soul was filled with peace and gladness." Nowadays many a tourist motors through Switzerland without ever discovering the valley of Langnau; or, whirling past it, has no desire to rest under the shadow of the trees by that stream of pure water. Indeed, it would be foolish for the hurrying tourist to tarry there. He would not find in himself, as Longfellow did, a new peace and gladness; and besides, he might miss his dinner in Lucerne.

A clear transparency of spirit, an *anima candida* like Virgil's, an unvarying gentleness and dignity of behavior: these were the traits which endeared Longfellow to those who knew him. The delicacy of his literary tact was one secret of his welcome, but the deeper secret—though this too was an open one—lay in the beauty of his character. There could be no better illustration of this than the familiar story of the pathetic but perfect tribute paid by Emerson, who, broken by age, and with a memory that had almost lapsed, attended Longfellow's funeral. They had been friends for nearly forty years. "I do not remember the name of the gentleman whose funeral we have attended," he said; "but he had a beautiful soul."

Those of us who once begged for Mr. Longfellow's autograph, or besieged, shyly or brazenly, the always open door of his home, can do no more than transmit our own impression of his personality. The coming generations will select their own poets, in obedience to some instinct which cannot be divined by us. For myself, I have no doubt that Americans, in a far-distant future, will look back to the author of "Evangeline" and "Hiawatha" as we look back to his favorite Walter von der Vogelweide, a Meistersinger of a golden age. Now and again, very likely, he may be neglected. He is already thought negligible by some clever young men of over-educated mind and under-educated heart, who borrow their ethics from the cavemen, their pragmatic philosophy from the drifting raft-men, and who, in the presence of the same material from which Longfellow wrought delightful poetry,—the same land-scape, the same rich past and ardent present and all the "long thoughts" of youth,— are themselves impotent to produce a single line.

But Longfellow's reputation may be trusted to safer hands than theirs. There can be no happier fortune than that which has made him the children's poet. These wise little people know so well what they like! They are untrou-bled with scruples and hesitancies. With how sure an instinct do they feel—without com-prehending or analyzing—the note of true poetry! Will Stevenson be one of the enduring writers? I look at his twenty-five volumes in shining red and gold, and cannot tell; but when I hear a child murmuring "My Shadow," I think I know. If there were a language for such childish secrets, the sweet voices that recite with delicious solemnity "The Children's Hour" might tell us more about Longfellow than we professional critics — with our meticulous

pedantry, our scrutiny of " sources," our ears
so trained to detect over-tones that we lose the
melody — shall ever learn.

The children go to the heart of the matter.
And so do many of those larger children — the
men and women of simple soul who keep an
unsophisticated way of looking at the world.
There are some very highly organized persons
who amuse themselves with poetry as they
would with chess, or Comparative Religion, or
" The Shaving of Shagpat." They can criticise
and expound verses, and invent theories of po-
etics, and compile anthologies. But these val-
uable members of the intellectual community
are not the real readers of poetry. To find the
true audience of a Heine, a Tennyson, a Longfellow, you are not to look in the Social Regis-
ter. You must seek out the shy boy and girl
who live on dull streets and hill roads — no
matter where, so long as the road to dreamland
leads from their gate; you must seek the work-
ing-girls and shopkeepers, the " schoolteachers
and country ministers" who put and kept Longfellow's friend Sumner in the Senate; you must
make a census of the lonely, uncounted souls
who possess the treasures of the humble. These

readers are sadly ignorant of Ibsen and Bernard Shaw and Fogazzaro; but when the conversation shifts to Shakespeare they brighten up. They know their Shakespeare, and they know Longfellow. They are sometimes described as the intellectual "middle class"; but a poet may well say, as a President of the United States once said of a camp-meeting at Ocean Grove, "Give me the support of those people, and I can snap my fingers at the rest."

It is folly to worship numbers. But it is a deeper folly not to perceive that among the uncritical masses there may be a right instinct for the essence of poetry. It is glory enough for Longfellow that he is read by the same persons who still read Robert Burns and the Plays of Shakespeare and the English Bible. Until simplicity and reverence go wholly out of fashion he will continue to be read. In that quaint Flemish city which Longfellow's verses have helped to make famous there is a tiny room, in the Hospital of St. John, in which are treasured some of the loveliest pictures of Hans Memling. The years come and go, in Bruges; the streets and canals grow quieter here, noisier there, than they used to be; the belfry that

Longfellow admired looks down to-day on advertisements of Sunlight Soap and American Petroleum. Yet in that hushed room in the inner courtyard of the Hospital, visitors still linger entranced, as of old, over Memling's Marriage of St. Catherine, his Adoration of the Magi, and his Shrine of St. Ursula. Purity of color and of line are there, delicate brush-work, a charming fancy, a clear serenity of spirit; they are masterpieces of a born painter whose nature was also that of the dreamer, the story-teller, the devotee. There are Venetian and Roman painters far greater than Hans Memling. And there are poets whose strength of wing and fiery energy of imagination are beyond Longfellow's. But no truer poet ever lived.

Thomas Bailey Aldrich

Thomas Bailey Aldrich

On the day when he last entered the Atlantic office, in January, 1907, Mr. Aldrich seemed, for the first time, to have grown old. One of his friends spoke of it, as he went out. Up to that morning, the weight of seventy years had scarcely seemed to touch the erect, jaunty figure. The lines that time had written around his clear blue eyes and firm mouth conveyed no hint of senility. His hair was scarcely gray. His voice, slightly husky in its graver, sweeter tones, retained a delicious youthful crispness as it curled and broke, wave-like, into flashing raillery. He had just completed his poem for the Longfellow centenary, his first verse after some years of silence; and when it was praised to his face — for who could help praising it! — he blushed with pleasure like a boy. Yet he had passed three-score and ten, and the shadow, invisible as yet and quite unheralded, was drawing very near.

[143]

For many years he had been wont to visit more or less regularly the editorial room which still claimed his name and fame as one of its treasured possessions. Perched upon the edge of a chair, as if about to take flight, he would often linger by the hour, to the delight of his listeners. His caustic wit played around every topic of conversation. He did not disdain the veriest "shop-talk" concerning printers' errors and the literary fashions of the hour. "Look at those boys!" he exclaimed once, as he picked up an illustrated periodical containing the portraits of a couple of that month's beardless novelists. "When I began to write, we waited twenty years before we had our pictures printed; but nowadays these young fellows have themselves photographed before they even sit down to write their book." Himself a fastidious composer and reviser, Mr. Aldrich was severely critical of current magazine literature. "That was a well-written essay," he once said of an Atlantic contribution which he liked, "but you will find that you used a superfluous 'of' upon the second page." It was very rarely that he praised a contemporary poem. Mr. S. V. Cole's "In Via Merulana" and some of the exquisite lyrics

[144]

of Father Tabb are the only verses of recent years which I now recall as having won his unqualified approbation. More than once I have heard him declare that he would have rejected Mr. Kipling's "Recessional" if it had been offered to the Atlantic, — so extreme was his dislike for one or two harsh lines in that justly celebrated poem. The one American poem which he would have most liked to write, was, he said, Emerson's "Bacchus," — where, amid inimitable felicities, there are surely harsh lines enough.

One of the most pleasant traits of Mr. Aldrich's comments upon men of letters was his unfailing respect and admiration for the well-known group of New England writers whose personal friendship he had enjoyed. His gift for witty derogation found employment elsewhere; towards Emerson, Longfellow, Whittier, and Lowell his attitude was finely reverent, as befitted a younger associate. He was fond of retelling that anecdote of his own boyish daring which appears in his "Ponkapog Papers," to the effect that when first entering James T. Fields's office in the Old Corner Bookstore, his eyes fell upon that kindly editor and pub-

lisher's memorandum book, open on the table.
Mr. Fields was absent for the moment, and the
youthful poet could not help noticing the impressive list of *agenda:* "Don't forget to mail
R. W. E. his contract,"—"Don't forget O.
W. H.'s proofs," etc. Whereupon the "young
Milton," who certainly deserved to succeed in
his profession, wrote upon the memorandum
book, "Don't forget to accept T. B. A.'s poem,"
and disappeared. The poem was accepted, paid
for, and, truest kindness of all,—as Mr. Aldrich asserted,—was never printed. But the
resourceful youth never lost his deferential attitude toward the bearers of those famous ini-
tialed names that had once preceded his own.

Of his early literary friendships with the New
York set of writers in his "Home Journal" and
"Mirror" days he often talked entertainingly,
and in a freer vein. He knew Whitman, for
example, and liked him personally, although he
would never admit that Whitman was a poet
except by virtue of here and there a single
phrase. Many a time has the present writer en-
deavored to convert Mr. Aldrich from this state
of heathen blindness as to Whitman's genius,
but the debates used to end illogically with Mr.

Aldrich's delightful story of a certain nine dollars which Whitman once borrowed from him — magnificently, but alas, irrevocably — in Pfaff's genial restaurant on Broadway. Never did Aldrich appear more truly the poet than in these light reminiscent touches upon the varied adventures of his youth. He had gone out against the Philistines armed with no weapon except a finely pointed pen. He had written no line dishonorably, or unworthily of his craftsman's conscience. He had compelled recognition, and taken his seat unchallenged among the choicest company of American men of letters. It amused him to look back upon his early career as a struggling journalist, to

> Chirp over days in a garret,
> Chuckle o'er increase of salary,
> Taste the good fruits of our leisure,
> Talk about pencil and lyre, —
> And the National Portrait Gallery.

He neither forgot nor forgave some of his old antagonists in that journalistic world ; but one liked him all the better for the sensitiveness of nature which left him still resentful of some ancient slight, or still happily mindful of a compliment earned when he was twenty. Few of the "irritable tribe" of poets could, however, keep themselves more perfectly in hand. The cool audacity of his "Don't forget to accept T. B. A.'s poem" ripened into an easy mastery of many of the arts of life. His gay confidence, when seated among his friends or guests, reminded one of some veteran commander of an ocean liner, enjoying, at the head of the "captain's table," the deserved deference of the company.

Yet he seemed the poet, likewise, in his air of detachment from the immediate concerns of the people who surrounded him. Thrown by force of circumstances, in his later life, into the agreeable society of the idle rich, he got and gave such pleasures as are only there obtainable; but he never abdicated his essential citizenship among the dreamers and artists. That he would have produced more printer's "copy" under the spur of harsh necessity is easily demonstrable, but it does not follow that this conceivably ampler production would have exhibited any finer quality than is now found in the prose and verse of his collected works. He once wrote some suggestive verses on "The Flight of the Goddess," — the fickle muse who

[148]

loves poets in their garret days and deserts them in prosperity. But these verses do not demand an autobiographical interpretation. Mr. Aldrich's own muse was of a long constancy. At nineteen he proved his kinship with the rarest spirits of his time, and for the next half-century there was no year when his friends and readers would not have spoken of him primarily as a maker of poetry. He always kept some avenue of escape from the prosaic. In his boyhood at Portsmouth the sea was ever at the end of the street:—

> I leave behind me the elm-shadowed square
> And carven portals of the silent street,
> And wander on with listless, vagrant feet,
> Through seaward-leading alleys, till the air
> Smells of the sea, and straightway then the care
> Slips from my heart, and life once more is sweet.
> At the lane's ending lie the white-winged fleet.
> O restless Fancy, whither wouldst thou fare?
> Here are brave pinions that shall take thee far —
> Gaunt hulks of Norway; ships of red Ceylon;
> Slim-masted lovers of the blue Azores!
> 'T is but an instance hence to Zanzibar,
> Or to the regions of the Midnight Sun;
> Ionian isles are thine, and all the fairy shores!

Besides this sea-longing, so inbred in the natives of New England seaport towns, there was some delicate strand of foreignness among the ancestral fibres of Aldrich's nature, his heritage from that

> creature soft and fine,
> From Spain, some say, some say from France,

whom he has described in the lines entitled "Heredity." He touches this thought again in his sonnet "Reminiscence" : —

> Though I am native to this frozen zone
> That half the twelvemonth torpid lies, or dead;
> Though the cold azure arching overhead
> And the Atlantic's never-ending moan
> Are mine by heritage, I must have known
> Life otherwhere in epochs long since fled;
> For in my veins some Orient blood is red,
> And through my thought are lotus blossoms strown.

It was fitting that three years of his impressionable youth should have been passed in the New Orleans of the forties, where the rich coloring of the past still lingered, and where, though Cotton was striving to be king, Romance was queen. When the boy was brought back to Portsmouth to prepare for college, he had become, as "The Story of a Bad Boy" humorously portrays, the veriest Southern fire-

eater. His counting-room experiences in New
York — which followed the abandonment of
his college career upon his father's death in
1849 — also brought him into touch with ways
of life quite alien to those of his New Hampshire birthplace. Before he was twenty he had
graduated from the counting-room into the
Broadway school of journalists and poets, and
had issued his first volume of verse, " The
Bells, by T. B. A." This was in 1855, the
year of Whittier's " Barefoot Boy " and Whitman's " Leaves of Grass." Aldrich's first volume is now a rarity, and all of its nearly fifty
pieces — with their echoes of Chatterton, Tom
Moore, Poe, and Longfellow — have disappeared from the standard editions of his Poems.

Two years later, in November, 1857, appeared the first number of the Atlantic
Monthly. I have before me a yellowing note
written by Aldrich, in the following May, to
F. H. Underwood, who was then acting as
Lowell's assistant upon the magazine. Underwood, at his chief's request,[1] had returned one
of Aldrich's poems with some suggestions as
to changes in wording.

[1] Lowell's letter to Underwood is printed on p. 264.

PARK-STREET PAPERS

HOME JOURNAL OFFICE, May 25, 1858.

DEAR SIR, — I have been trying for the last hour to alter the "Blue Bell" verses. "Mute worshipers of Christ" is simply bad; but "dawning" and "morning" form a perfect rhyme when we remember the "*fancies*" and "*pansies*" of the old poets. It has taken you some time to find out that such rhymes are inadmissible; but you seem to have good authority in the following *pasquinade*, which I clip from the "Boston Post" of May 24: —

Poet.　　　　I 'm sure I have an ear!
Editor.　No doubt! — I 've known a poet with a pair,
　　　And very long ones — who was not aware
　　　That ʻmornʼ and ʻdawnʼ have not the proper chime,
　　　By a long shot, to make a decent rhyme.

As I cannot make the changes you require, I shall, of course, retain my verses.

　　　　　Yours, etc.,
　　　　　　T. B. ALDRICH.

Mr. F. H. UNDERWOOD.

Having thus vindicated his dignity, the youthful bard, who was himself assistant editor of the "Home Journal," apparently continued to reflect upon the Atlantic's suggestion. But he did not yield at once. In the Carleton edition of his Poems, 1863, "The Blue Bells of New England" contains the erring stanza:—

> All night your eyes are closed in sleep,
> But open at the dawning;
> Such simple faith as yours can see
> God's coming in the morning.

In the Ticknor and Fields' Blue and Gold edition of 1865, however, the second line of the stanza becomes

> Kept fresh for day's *adorning,*

no doubt to Mr. Underwood's satisfaction. Aldrich's first poetical contribution to the Atlantic was "Pythagoras," in June, 1860; his first story, which excited Hawthorne's curiosity as to the author, and prompted some beautiful words of praise from the romancer, was " Père Antoine's Date-Palm: a Legend of New Orleans," in June, 1862.

The letter to Underwood reveals one trait which Aldrich possessed in common with Tennyson, his chief master and guide in the art of poetry. Both men were quick to profit by adverse criticism. Some American scholar will ultimately, no doubt, edit Aldrich's youthful poems, as Mr. Churton Collins has edited the earliest work of Tennyson, with the aim of showing, by means of the successive verbal alterations, the tireless patience and acquired cunning of the born craftsman in verse. The files of the Atlantic will yield him two striking illustrations, drawn from Aldrich's maturer work. In December, 1874, Edgar Fawcett, in reviewing his poems, quoted approvingly "The Lunch," — a dozen lines of *genre* painting in the Keats-Tennyson manner, closing as follows: —

Two China cups with golden tulips sunny,
And rich inside with chocolate like honey;
And she and I the banquet-scene completing
With dreamy words, — and very pleasant eating!

The critic remarked that the last four words marred the spirit of ethereal daintiness till then so deliciously apparent. Whereupon Mr. Aldrich, with the happiest aptitude for taking second thought, substituted the present version of the last line, —

With dreamy words, *and fingers shyly meeting*.

Again, in January, 1877, Mr. Howells, whose unsigned Atlantic criticisms of Aldrich's successive volumes are models of friendly tact and delicate instruction, quoted the quatrain "Masks": —

[154]

Thomas Bailey Aldrich

Black Tragedy lets slip her grim disguise
And shows you laughing lips and roguish eyes;
But when, unmasked, gay Comedy appears,
'T is ten to one you find the girl in tears.

Mr. Howells suggested that the strong effect in the last line was weakened by what seemed to him a mistaken colloquiality; and in the "Complete Poems" the line now reads,—

How wan her cheeks are, and what heavy tears.

We must not linger over such details. They will serve for concrete illustration of the qualities which made Aldrich respected and admired by his fellow-writers. By 1865, the year of his marriage and removal to Boston as the editor of "Every Saturday" for Ticknor and Fields, he was already widely known as the author of refined and tender verse, as a capable and shrewd editorial worker, and as a clever man of the world. His new employers printed his Poems in one of their celebrated Blue and Gold editions. For the latitude of Boston this was comparable to an election to the French Academy. Aldrich was not yet thirty. Rarely has there been a more fortunate Return of the Native. And nevertheless, although he was to be identified with Boston henceforward until the end

of his life, he was never to lose his engaging air
of detachment from New England's cherished
enterprises. He cared no more for the practical
later phases of Transcendentalism than for the
earlier speculative ones. The various "re-
forms," philanthropies, "causes," of his excellent neighbors did not interest him deeply.
The intellectual and social evolution of New
England in the last quarter of the nineteenth
century is not to be traced in his poetry or his
prose. His favorite reading at the time of his
Atlantic editorship was French novels. The
sombre inland New England of our own school
of short-story writers, — the gaunt pastures, the
lonely white farm-houses, the fierce emotional
energy, the tragedies of baffled will and thwarted
natural instincts, — all this was foreign to the
happy sensuousness of his nature.

The fifteen years following 1865 were Aldrich's most productive period. For nine years
he edited "Every Saturday." He wrote for
"Our Young Folks" the most popular of all
his books, that "Story of a Bad Boy" in which
Portsmouth is pictured under the name of
Rivermouth, and Tom Bailey is but the thin-
nest of disguises for the youthful Aldrich. Some

of the Atlantic's present readers remember waiting eagerly for the next installment of "The Bad Boy"; if they will read it over again, after an interval of nearly forty years, they will find that Binny Wallace's drifting out to sea has lost nothing of its pathos, and that the fight between Tom Bailey and Conway is just as glorious a combat as of old. Aldrich's technique as a writer of the short story has not been excelled by that of any American, even by Poe, although he ventured upon no daring atmospheric effects and did not go far afield for his characters. He loved to mystify the inexperienced reader, and he arranged some neatly surprising dénoûments. "Marjorie Daw," his best-known short story, is a classic example of this swift and astonishing "curtain." "There is n't any Marjorie Daw!" Neither is there any Miss Mehetable's Son ; Mademoiselle Olympe Zabriski is a youth whose beard is getting too much for him; the fierce "Goliath" turns out to be a little panting tremulous wad of a lap-dog; "Our new neighbors at Ponkapog" are only a pair of orioles; and the charming Mrs. Rose Mason of "Two Bites at a Cherry" proves, to the consternation of both hero and reader,

to have married again! Aldrich was too clever
a workman to rely exclusively upon his favorite
method. "A Sea Turn," one of his latest stories, is a flawless handling of the comedy of
situation; he wrote humorous and pathetic character sketches in the style of Irving and Hawthorne; and in "Quite So" and "The White
Feather" he touches with admirable restraint
upon poignant tragedies of the Civil War.

"Prudence Palfrey," "The Queen of Sheba,"
and "A Stillwater Tragedy" — all of which
first appeared as Atlantic serials — exhibit Aldrich's deft mastery of prose and his skill in
composing a species of tale halfway between
romance and actuality. "Semi-idyllic" was Mr.
Howells's word for "Prudence Palfrey" in
1874; "in fact," he added, "the New England *novel* does not exist." "A Modern Instance" and "The Rise of Silas Lapham" had
not then been written. Whatever one may
think of the intellectual or imaginative limitations of the type of fiction which Aldrich here
attempted, the details of these longer stories
are wrought with the artistry of a poet. Ride
out of Rivermouth on a June morning with
Edward Lynde: "Now and then, as he passed

[158]

a farm house, a young girl hanging out clothes in the front yard — for it was on a Monday — would pause with a *shapeless snowdrift* in her hand to gaze curiously at the apparition of a gallant young horseman." This is no longer Rockingham County, New Hampshire; we are in Arcadia. Some connoisseur of women ought to collect the adorable vignettes that are scattered everywhere through Aldrich's prose; Marjorie Daw in the hammock, swaying "like a pond-lily in the golden afternoon"; Martha Hilton, "with a lip like a cherry and a cheek like a tea-rose"; Margaret Slocum's eyes, "fringed with such heavy lashes that the girl seemed always to be in half-mourning"; Mrs. Rose Mason, with her "long tan-colored gloves — Rue de la Paix" — in the chill and gloom of the Naples Cathedral; Anglice, "a blonde girl, with great eyes and a voice like the soft notes of a vesper hymn"; or young Mrs. Newbury, "looking distractingly cool and edible — something like celery — in her widow's weeds." All of Aldrich — save what is disclosed upon the highest levels of his poetry — is in that witty, charming, delicately sensuous description of young Mrs. Newbury. No other prose written in his generation has quite the same combination of qualities; but if Alphonse Daudet had been born in Portsmouth and compelled to write serials for a decorous Boston magazine, Aldrich might have found a rival in his own field.

It was to this matured and versatile talent that the conduct of the Atlantic Monthly was intrusted, upon Mr. Howells's resignation in 1881. For nine years Mr. Aldrich sat in his tiny editorial room overlooking the Granary Burying Ground, reading manuscripts, scanning proof-sheets, — though he delegated more of this drudgery than his contributors supposed, — and making witty remarks to his assistant. He had the comforts — both before and since his time considered too Capuan for an Atlantic editor in office hours — of a pipe and a red Irish setter. Once the setter ate up a sonnet. "How should *he* know it was doggerel?" exclaimed Mr. Aldrich compassionately. He had leisure for frequent travel abroad, and for the cementing of many delightful friendships. Peculiarly happy in his home life, he cultivated a gracious hospitality. His editorial reign, as one looks back upon it, was not so much Capuan

as Saturnian. The Literature of Exposure had
not yet been born, and the manners of the
market-place were not thought good form in
magazine offices. Mr. Aldrich printed poems
by Longfellow, Holmes, Whittier, Lowell,
Dante Rossetti, Stedman, and Sill, with an
occasional lyric of his own. Henry James,
Thomas Hardy, Miss Murfree, Arthur S.
Hardy, Miss Jewett, Elizabeth Stuart Phelps,
Marion Crawford, and Mrs. Oliphant were
among the writers of fiction. John Burroughs
and Bradford Torrey wrote outdoor papers.
Parkman and Fiske contributed historical articles. Now and then appeared articles by
H. D. Lloyd, Edward Atkinson, Richard T.
Ely, Laurence Laughlin, and Walter H. Page,
in token that the "age of economists," which
Burke dreaded, was close at hand. But the dis-
tinctive note of the Atlantic in the eighties was
its literary criticism, contributed by a group of
reviewers who often preferred to write anony-
mously. Their criticisms maintained a more se-
vere standard than that of any critical periodical
in the country except the "Nation," and they
exhibited a combination of learning with ur-
banity, which, with the present development

of specialization among scholars, seems to be growing more and more rare.

It would be idle to search the eighteen volumes of the Atlantic edited by Mr. Aldrich for any very plain indication of his personality, except his fondness for clear, competent, and workmanlike writing. Contributions poured into his little office, and he made such selections as he saw fit. It was before the day of Wild West feats of editorial chase, capture, and exhibition. The Atlantic was like a stanch ship sailing a well-charted course, and Aldrich, who was fond enough of salt water and knew how to steer, took his trick at the wheel with pleasure. Some of the unkindly necessities incident to his vocation naturally irritated him. He disliked to give pain. " Here goes for making twenty more enemies," he was wont to say as he sat down in the morning at his desk. When urged by the present writer to prepare some account of his editorship for the fiftieth anniversary number of the Atlantic, he said that if he told anything he would like to tell the story of the warlike contributor who once threatened him with personal violence, but who, upon being challenged by the editor to appear at Park Street to make good his threat, failed to come to time. As Mr. Aldrich described this imminent encounter of a score of years ago, his blue eyes flashed fire, and one could see little Tom Bailey, with both eyes blinded by big Conway, standing up to him, and thrashing him too, on the playground at Rivermouth. Here is the contributor's letter, preserved by Mr. Aldrich and printed at his desire.

T. B. ALDRICH,
    Editor of The Atlantic Monthly,
        No. 4 Park Street,
            Boston.

SIR:—On the 24th day of February and again on the 7th inst. I gave you opportunity to apologize for the willfully offensive manner in which you treated me in relation to my manuscript entitled *Shakespeare's Viola.*

You retained that manuscript *nearly seven weeks.* Then you returned it and expressed your *regret that you could not accept* it.

That is to say, you intended to deceive me by the inference that the *manuscript was declined on its merits.*

The truth was and is you did not read it *nor*

even open the package. Therefore you could not judge its merits nor say, with truth, that you regretted to decline it.

You decline to apologize.

My robust nature abhors your disgusting duplicity. You are a vulgar, unblushing Rascal and an impudent audacious *Liar*.

Which I am prepared to maintain any *where*, any *time*. You ought to be publicly horse-whipped. Nothing would gratify me more than to give you a sounder thrashing than any *you have yet received*.

Moreover I am determined that the Literary Public shall know what a putrid *scoundrel* and *Liar* you *are*.

Boston, March 30, 1887.

Then follows, in Aldrich's beautiful open handwriting, the penciled comment: "The gentleman with the 'robust nature' was politely invited to call at No. 4 Park St. on any day that week between 9 A. M. and 3 P. M.; but the 'robust nature' failed to materialize."

One smiles at such things, of course; but now that Mr. Aldrich is gone from the places that

once knew him, it is these trivialities, rather than
his accomplishment and his fame, that come first
to the mind. Perhaps it is the very security of
his fame which lends to these anecdotal memories of his editorship a sort of ironic relief.
"The power of writing one fine line," said
Edward FitzGerald, "transcends all the Able-
Editor ability in the ably-edited universe."
Aldrich wrote not merely one fine line, but hundreds of them, and it is inconceivable that they
will all pass out of human memory. Time, which
is sure to winnow so sternly the work of the more
famous New England poets, will find that Aldrich has done most of the winnowing himself.
The text of his "Complete Poems" represents
his own final choice of what was most excellent.
In his lighter vein he was acknowledged to be
unrivaled upon this side of the water. But even
the fairylike daintiness of "Latakia," "Cory-
don," "At a Reading," "Pampina," "Palabras
Cariñosas," and "A Petition," or the pure lyri-
cism of "A Nocturne," "Pillared Arch," "I 'll
not confer with Sorrow," and "Imogen," and
still more the popular "Baby Bell," — written,
like Rossetti's "Blessed Damozel," at nineteen,
— fail to represent the full power of his ripened

mind and art. There is a deeper note in his lines
in memory of Bayard Taylor and upon Booth's
portrait, in "Sea-Longings," "At the Funeral
of a Minor Poet," and the startling verses,
"Identity." The darker questionings that occasionally shadowed the sunny Greek sky of
Aldrich's fancy are reflected in "An Untimely
Thought," "Apparitions," and "Prescience."
No American poet save Longfellow has written such perfect sonnets as "I vex me not,"
"Sleep," "Fredericksburg," "Enamored ar-
chitect of airy rhyme," "Andromeda," and
others not inferior to these. Indifferent as he
was toward public affairs, the memories of the
Civil War inspired two of his elegiac pieces,
"Spring in New England" and the "Ode on
the Shaw Memorial." He was stirred to the composition of a fine sonnet upon reading William
Watson's splendid poetical invective against the
Armenian outrages. "Unguarded Gates" was
the result of many weeks of excitement, quite
unusual with him, over the national dangers involved in unrestricted immigration. But these
were almost his only excursions into the field
of communal verse, whether political or social.
The one great personal sorrow of his life, the

death of his son Charles in 1904, came after his work as a poet was finished.

Aldrich wrote Tennysonian blank verse with consummate skill, as may be seen in "Wyndham Towers," "White Edith," and other narrative pieces. His Oriental poetry is picturesque, but, like Mrs. Rose Mason's gloves, suggests the Rue de la Paix, — or at least Horace Vernet and Fromentin. His wit, his cleverness of phrase, his keen sense of the comic, and his life-long interest in the stage and stage-folk, might have made him, one would think, an unexcelled writer of comedies. Yet his chief ventures in dramatic composition — aside from some early unpreserved fragments — are tragedies. "Mercedes," as played by Julia Arthur, was a notable performance, although narrow in its range of dramatic forces. "Judith of Bethulia," a dramatized version of his early narrative poem "Judith and Holofernes," was an experiment which brought new zest into his closing years. The play was skillfully put together, and its third act was powerful, but it was acted, on the first night at least, with a crude commonness that failed alike to do justice to Aldrich's rich lines and to compel the admiration of the indifferent play-

[167]

goer. The failure of the play was a pity, yet one may question whether a success would have made any difference in the total impression left by Aldrich upon his generation.

In reviewing his latest volumes of prose for the Atlantic,[1] I ventured to apply to Mr. Aldrich a sentence from his own charming essay upon Herrick: "A fine thing incomparably said instantly becomes familiar, and has henceforth a sort of dateless excellence." The secret of that dateless excellence was possessed by Aldrich himself. To judge merely by their mood, many of his poems might have been written in the garden of Herrick's Devon parsonage, or a whole century later, upon the sloping lawn of Horace Walpole's villa of Strawberry Hill. Aldrich would have been a delightful companion for George Selwyn and Harry Montague, and he could also have joyously discussed the art of polishing verse and prose with Théophile Gautier and Prosper Mérimée. His spirit escapes the rigid limits set by the biographical dictionary. In his choice of metrical forms and his vocabulary he is obviously indebted to Tennyson's volume of 1842, yet it is usually im-

[1] In November, 1903.

[168]

possible to determine by internal evidence —
as one often can in Tennyson's case — in what
decade of the nineteenth century his various
poems were written. The general trend of the
philosophical, religious, or political speculation
of Aldrich's day is not discoverable in his work.
He had no such ethical and doctrinaire preoc-
cupations as colored the verse of Whittier and
Arnold, and troubled, though it sometimes
strangely exalted, the later lyrics of Tennyson.
Aldrich's poetry, like that of Keats and Rossetti, is free from the alloy of essentially unpoetical elements; it bears no traces of *Tendenz;*
its excellence is dateless.

In this tranquil aloofness from the passions
and convictions of the hour, and in the beautiful
perfection of its workmanship, lies its promise
of long life. There will always be some readers
who are no more likely to forget Aldrich's
poetry than Mozart's music or the crocus
breaking through the mould in March. The
very lightest of his pieces, marked "Fragile"
as they are, are dear to the spirit of beauty, and
will possess something of the perpetually renewed immortality of the cobwebs sparkling
on the lawn and the fairy frostwork on the pane.

And yet, if one were to choose where no choice
is needful, one might hazard the guess that the
hearts of future readers are more likely, as the
years go by, to be turned toward the few poems
in which Aldrich has deepened the wistful
beauty of his lines by thoughts of the mysteries
which encompass us. Whether he pondered
often upon such themes one cannot tell, but one
likes to think of him, at the last, as sustained
by the noble mood in which he composed his
final sonnet:—

> I vex me not with brooding on the years
> That were ere I drew breath: why should I then
> Distrust the darkness that may fall again
> When life is done? Perchance in other spheres —
> Dead planets — I once tasted mortal tears,
> And walked as now amid a throng of men,
> Pondering things that lay beyond my ken,
> Questioning death, and solacing my fears.
> Ofttimes indeed strange sense have I of this,
> Vague memories that hold me with a spell,
> Touches of unseen lips upon my brow,
> Breathing some incommunicable bliss!
> In years foregone, O Soul, was all not well?
> Still lovelier life awaits thee. Fear not thou!

WHITTIER FOR TO-DAY

Whittier for To-day

WHITTIER was born in 1807, the year of Byron's "Hours of Idleness." During the year
following, the English army in the Peninsular
War, allied with the forces of Spain and Portu-
gal, made what the poet Wordsworth felt to
be a shameful treaty with the French. In his
pamphlet against this Convention of Cintra,
Wordsworth justified, with passionate elo-
quence, the right of noble-minded men to assert themselves in times of moral tumult and
confused political aims. He pictured the human soul "breaking down limit, and losing and
forgetting herself in the sensation and image of
Country and the human race." In such crises,
he declared, the emotions transcend the immediate object which excites them. War, terrible
in its naked cruelty, yet "attracting the more
benign by the accompaniment of some shadow
which seems to sanctify it; the senseless weav-

[173]

ing and interweaving of factions — vanishing
and reviving and piercing each other like the
Northern Lights; public commotions, and
those in the breast of the individual; . . . these
demonstrate that the passions of men (I mean
the soul of sensibility in the heart of man) do
immeasurably transcend their objects. The true
sorrow of humanity consists in this: not that
the mind of man fails, but that the course and
demands of action and of life so rarely corre-
spond with the dignity and intensity of human
desires."

Clouded as these words are with excess of
feeling, few passages could suggest more vividly
one function which Whittier's poetry was to
fulfill. Gifted with far less genius than either
Wordsworth or Byron, Whittier nevertheless
felt "public commotions" as profoundly as
did either of the English poets. He guided the
passionate feeling of his faction and party more
definitely than they, and to a more successful
issue. The "demands of action" matched the
intensity of his desires. Confronting a specific
phase of the old question of human liberty, —
a question which faces every poet who reflects
upon man in his social relations, — Whittier

grew from a mere facile rhymester into a master
of political poetry. During the thirty years that
ended with the close of the Civil War, no
poetic voice in America was so potent as Whittier's in evoking and embodying the humanitarian spirit.

He continued to compose verse for nearly
thirty years after the conflict over Slavery had
been settled, and these later poems contributed
largely to his popularity. But his mind was
formed, his imagination kindled, and his hand
perfected, amid the fiery pressure of events.
He voiced not only those voiceless generations
of pioneers from which he sprang, but also the
dumb passion of sympathy, of indignation, of
loyalty, which was to swing vast armies of common men into march and battle. It was a curious destiny for the Quaker lad. Frail of body,
timid, poor, untaught, he had discovered on
reading Burns that he, too, had a poet's soul.
He learned from William Lloyd Garrison the
secret of losing one's life and saving it, so that
in becoming — in his own words — "a man
and not a mere verse-maker" he found in that
surrender to the claims of humanity the inspiration which transformed him into a poet.

[175]

Will our people continue to read him? At the death of Tennyson, which fell in the same year as Whittier's (1892), a decorous little company gathered in an American college town to read and discuss some of the Laureate's poetry. It was a grave and wholly edifying occasion. One of the company was a lawyer, then far advanced in age, of the highest professional standing, and the senior warden of his church. When the programme was completed and the ice cream was imminent, the stately old lawyer drew me cautiously behind a door.

"Do you really enjoy Tennyson?" he demanded.

"Yes," said I, in some surprise. "Don't you?"

"No!" he exclaimed. "It has too many involutions and convolutions for me. I don't like it. Did you ever read Byron's 'Marino Faliero'?"

"I was reading it only yesterday," said I.

The senior warden's eye kindled with sudden fire. "Well, *that's* the kind of poetry *I* like: *where the old man stands up and gives 'em hell!*" And with a friendly wink at me — a reader of the poet of his boyhood — the old

[176]

gentleman blandly joined one of the groups of
ladies who were still talking about

"laborious Orient ivory"

and

"the mellow ouzel fluting in the elm."

No coiner of literary phrases could have conveyed so effectively the nature of the spell once
cast over readers by Byron's passionate decla-
mation. The harangues of Faliero and Man-
fred and Cain are, if one pleases, rebel's rhetoric
rather than poetry, speech instead of song. Yet
they moved men once as no one is moved
to-day by any living writer of verse. Whittier
shared with Byron the faculty of forging at
white heat such stanzas as were instantly accepted as poetry. A later age is inclined to
classify them as pamphleteering or as oratory.
Lowell writes to Whittier to "cry aloud and
spare not against the accursed Texas plot," and
Whittier straightway composes his "Texas":

Up the hillside, down the glen,
Rouse the sleeping citizen ;
Summon out the might of men!

Aside from its use of metre and rhyme, it might
be one of Lowell's own anti-slavery editorials.

[177]

Whittier's stout-hearted sea-captain, who declares : —

"Pile my ship with bars of silver, pack with coins of Spanish gold,
From keel-piece up to deck-plank, the roomage of the hold.
By the living God who made me! — I would sooner in your bay
Sink ship and crew and cargo, than bear this child away!"

is scarcely distinguishable from Garrison asseverating: —

"I am in earnest — I will not equivocate — I will not excuse — I will not retreat a single inch — *and I will be heard*." Both are honest men, aflame with righteous indignation ; neither is a poet. Just as Elliott's "Corn Law Rhymes" are often but a metrical version of the speeches of Cobden and Bright, so Whittier's anti-slavery verse is sometimes but a rhythmical rearrangement of matter that would have served equally well for a peroration by Wendell Phillips or a leader by Horace Greeley. The aim of them all was to inform, to explain, to call to action ; and a half-century after the action is over, the rhymes, like the speech and the article, are likely to share the pamphlet's fate. All have served their hour.

Many of Whittier's political poems, however, refuse to be disposed of thus easily. Their material still seems to be the stuff from which enduring poetry is wrought. Defects of workmanship may mar their surface, but the imaginative fabric is essentially unimpaired. The force of his ideas and sentiments far outweighs the deficiencies in technical craftsmanship. His antislavery poetry is based upon certain convictions, familiar enough to all who know the facts of Whittier's life. He inherited a love of freedom as an abstract notion — "the faith in which my father stood" — and a corresponding hatred of kingcraft and priestcraft. The movement for abolition in England and America seemed to him, as to his father, a legitimate consequence of the principles which had triumphed in the French Revolution. He was endowed with warm human feeling. His loyalty to the bonds of family, neighborhood, and state was absolute, and he merged this loyalty, without impairing it, into what Wordsworth called "the sensation and image of Country and the human race."

Add to this poetic capital an intimate knowledge of the men of his section, a shrewd political eye for the currents of public opinion, a com-

mand of simple, racy, fervent speech, the self-
possession of a Quaker and "come-outer," and
a high courageous heart,—and you have an
almost ideal image of a poet armed and ready
in a noble cause.

To appreciate Whittier's moral courage is
difficult without a precise knowledge of the sort
of ostracism which he faced. A physician in
Washington, Dr. Crandall, languished in prison
until he contracted a fatal illness, under sentence for the misdemeanor of reading a borrowed copy of Whittier's pamphlet " Justice
and Expediency." No anarchist to-day is a
more "unsafe" person in the eyes of respectable society than were the Abolitionists. Your

> Solid man of Boston;
> A comfortable man, with dividends,
> And the first salmon, and the first green peas,

was irritated by Whittier then as he is irritated
by Gorky to-day.

In the eyes of the typical commercial circles
of Massachusetts, Whittier was for twenty years
an agitator and therefore an outcast. The idol
of that society was Daniel Webster; and Whittier, with a scorn and sorrow all the more ter-

rible for its recognition of Webster's high powers, described him in 1850 as an Ichabod:—

> from those great eyes
> The soul has fled:
> When faith is lost, when honor dies,
> The man is dead!

A year later, in the poem to Kossuth, Webster's glorious voice—

> designed
> The bugle-march of Liberty to wind —

becomes merely

> the hoarse note of the bloodhound's baying,
> The wolf's long howl behind the bondman's flight.

Years afterward, it is true, in one of the most
touching of his poems, Whittier mourns that
Webster's august head was laid wearily down,—

> Too soon for us, too soon for thee,
> Beside thy lonely Northern sea.

But in the Titan's lifetime Whittier's words
were those of stern and sorrowful rebuke.

Nor did the social forces which supported
Webster fare better in Whittier's day of wrath.
In his "Stanzas for the Times" (1835) and
" Moloch in State Street," the

ancient sacrifice
Of Man to Gain

is denounced with prophetic sternness. In "The
Pine Tree" the conventional arguments of the
solid citizens of Boston are tossed aside as if
the old, reckless "Ça ira" wind were blowing.
The tune is,—

> Perish banks and perish traffic, spin your cotton's latest
> pound.

It is,—

> Tell us not of banks and tariffs, cease your paltry pedler
> cries;
> Shall the good State sink her honor that your gambling
> stocks may rise?

A Trust Company in Greater Boston chose
for its advertising motto, not long ago, the
phrase: "Banking, the Foundation of Government." Whittier would have smiled at that
placard with grim Jacobinical disdain.

Equally revolutionary was his attack upon
the clergy. Crosier and crown, to him, were
"twin-born vampires." Chief-priests and rulers
were conniving with each other, as of old. In
"Clerical Oppressors" Whittier cried,—

> Woe to the priesthood! woe
> To those whose hire is with the price of blood;

Perverting, darkening, changing, as they go,
　　The searching truths of God!

With bitter sarcasm in "The Pastoral Letter," with stinging invective in "The Christian Slave" and "The Sentence of John L. Brown," Whittier scourged the clerical upholders of the "divine institution." Finally, in "A Sabbath Scene," when the parson returns thanks to God for the capture of the fugitive slave girl, the poet can endure no more:—

My brain took fire: "Is this," I cried,
　"The end of prayer and preaching?
Then down with pulpit, down with priest,
　And give us Nature's teaching!"

This is the unadulterated doctrine of 1789. Pennsylvania Hall, the ill-starred Abolitionist headquarters in Philadelphia, is transformed in Whittier's imagination into the one

Temple sacred to the Rights of Man.

One is curious to know how many of the successors of the clergymen whom Whittier held up to obloquy read out his hymns to-day with any suspicion of the agony of soul, the despair for the priesthood and the church, in which many of those hymns were written.

It is needless to multiply illustrations of
Whittier's attitude toward the specific issue of
American slavery. To his mind this particular
battle was but one phase of the long humanitarian campaign against world-wide injustice.
Through the electric currents of his verse the
better aspirations of the eighteenth century and
even the phrases and the passions of European
Revolution were brought into contact with the
American conscience. But he was far more than
what he modestly described himself as being, a
mere

> Weapon in the war with wrong.

History and legend of Indian and colonist,
songs of homely labor, pictures of the Merri-
mac country-side, bits of foreign lore and fancy,
—all these alternate in Whittier's verse with
elegies over dead Abolitionists and stern sum-
monses to action. He read a great variety of
books and kept in close touch with the move-
ments of European politics. Although he never
went abroad, the names of Garibaldi, Thiers,
or Pius IX suggested to him themes for poems
as readily as did the personality of his friends
Fields and Sumner. He could turn out a Brown-
ingesque piece like "From Perugia," without

betraying the fact that he had never set foot
in Italy. His was not merely a home-keeping
mind or heart. Garrison's motto for the "Liber-
ator": "Our country is the world—our countrymen are mankind," spoke a sentiment which
permeates all of Whittier's verse like light. It
sustained him when the American outlook grew
dark; it sweetened and broadened his spirit.
From the later forties to the close of the Civil
War, it is instructive as well as pleasant to observe how many of his poetic themes are detached from the immediate emotions of the
hour. More and more he emerged from the atmosphere of faction and section. Even his poems
prompted by the war itself, like "Barbara Frietchie" and "Laus Deo," breathe a spirit of nationality and not of partisanship. The struggle had
scarcely ceased when he wrote "Snow-Bound,"
an idyllic composition which was instantly and
truly interpreted as an intimate revelation of
Whittier's real nature. He was almost sixty
when it appeared, and for the rest of his long life
he was known to his countrymen as the author
of "Snow-Bound." The old homestead at East
Haverhill is now visited by thousands of pilgrims who are more anxious to see "the clean-

winged hearth" and the stepping-stones by the brook than they are to rake the ashes from the old fires of the Abolition controversy.

So he grew old, a plain figure of a man, shrewd, gentle, loving the talk of gracious women, loving his summer glimpses of mountain and shore, and yet essentially lonely. He used to sit in the little back room of the Amesbury House, over a sheet-iron stove, and glance now at a photograph of the bust of Marcus Aurelius and now at the florid face of Henry Ward Beecher, on the opposite wall, — saying playfully that he was a sort of compromise between the two. The stoic was in his blood, certainly, and there was something, too, of the sentimentalist and the agitator. New Englanders, and especially the transplanted New Englanders of the West, loved him to the last, knowing him as only kinsmen can know one another. The rest of the country respected him for the uprightness of his long career, for his courage in the dark days, and for the fame which his verse had won. He died, at the great age of eighty-five, only fifteen years ago.

Only fifteen years, yet in the flux and change of our national life during that interval, Whittier seems already as far away as Longfellow, who died ten years earlier. Even Hawthorne, who died in 1864, is scarcely, as a personal figure, more remote. It was as a neighborhood poet that Whittier began his career, — a rural prodigy who without schooling could make such rhymes as pleased the ear of Newburyport and Haverhill. He continued throughout his life to produce the sort of verse which appealed, first of all, to his neighbors. But even the most casual visitor to Whittier-Land to-day is struck by the change in the poet's audience. Here and there, and notably between the Whittier homestead and Amesbury, the ancient farms remain intact. Some of them are owned, as in Whittier's youth, by Quakers. As one drives along the elm-shaded roads, there may still be seen in a few dooryards the little weather-stained shops for home shoe-making, with flower-gardens around them, and perhaps, at the window, a gray head bent over the bench, finishing some fine hand-work that will be taken to Haverhill to-morrow. But these old men — the men for whom Whittier wrote — are dying. Machine-work and foreign "help" — as they still say in Essex County — are making the old native industries superfluous. Along

[187]

the lines of the electric cars are new dwellings,
ugly to the eye, and rented by French Canadians,
Poles, Italians, Greeks. What should these immigrants know or care for the "pines on Ramoth Hill," though Ramoth Hill, under another name, be only over their shoulder? Their
children will read "Maud Muller" and "Barbara Frietchie" in school, but even they will
need an annotated edition of "Snow-Bound"
to tell them why a hearth should be "winged"
and what "pendent trammels" are, and "Turk's
head" andirons.

Read the editorials which Whittier was writing in 1844 for the mill-folk of Lowell, — an
educated, thrifty, ambitious class, — and then
walk along the streets of Lowell and Lawrence
to-day, in the endeavor to find a native New
England face. They have almost disappeared.
Massachusetts, which reckoned about one-fifth
of her population as foreign-born or children of
foreign-born in 1857, — when Whittier began
to write for the Atlantic, — now finds this class
of her citizens in the majority. To the men and
women for whom Whittier wrote, the Boston of
to-day would be a city of aliens. Only thirty-two
per cent of its population is Protestant. No im-

agination can picture the laboring men of New England sitting down to read Whittier's "Songs of Labor." The very tools have changed, and the spirit of Whittier's Drovers and Shoemakers and Lumbermen is incomprehensible to their successors. It is too late — and too foolish — to raise any Know-Nothing alarm. Far better these immigrants, as raw material for Democracy's wholesome task, than that exhausted strain of Puritan stock which lives querulously in the cities or grows vile in the hill-towns. It is no worse for Boston to be misgoverned by a clever Irishman than by some inefficient Brahmin of the Back Bay. But whether these changes in the population are welcomed or deplored, the fact is obvious that the local public upon which Whittier's poetry depended for its immediate audience has altered beyond recognition.

What is true of New England is true to a greater or less degree of the whole country. New men, new habits, new political notions, are in the saddle. That New England should have lost whatever ascendency she once possessed is not a matter of prime importance. That the country no longer looks to her for political or literary leadership is due to many causes which have nothing to do with Whittier. And nevertheless, his life and his poetry were so intimately identified with his section, that its loss of prestige in the nation affects the present assessment of Whittier's significance.

One must admit that from some points of view he remains, what he was at the beginning, —a "local" poet. In spite of the clear resonance with which he now and again struck the note of nationality, and in spite of his cosmopolitan curiosity about the world at large,—a curiosity felt, for that matter, by many an Essex County seafaring man of the vanished type, — Whittier never lost a sort of rusticity. One may like him all the better for it. It goes with his rôle, like the rusticity of Burns. Yet it seems now, as Burns's provincialism does not, to narrow the range of his influence as a poet.

Whittier was limited, too, in his physical capacity to perceive beauty and in his artistic power to interpret it. Color-blind and tune-deaf as he was, knowing no full and rich life of the body, his poetry is deficient in sensuous charm. Its passion is a moral passion only. With a natural facility in metre and rhyme, his workmanship betrayed throughout his career a carelessness for

literature as an art. His rhymes were often mere
improvised approximations. In one poem alone
he rhymes "God" with "abode," "word" and
"record." From the hundreds of still uncollected
poems which he scrawled in youth, down to the
jocose doggerel — never intended for publication — with which his old age sometimes relaxed
itself, Whittier exhibited little delicacy of ear,
little reverence for that instrument of verse on
which he had learned to play without a teacher.
He cared intensely for the feelings communi-
cated by the art of poetry, but he expressed more
than once in his letters a kind of contempt for
craftsmanship, for "literary reputation."

Even in that field of moral ideas where his
strength lay, his path was likewise narrow. Sternly, and as it proved victoriously, he brought the
teachings of the Old and New Testaments, as
freely interpreted by his own Quaker sect, to
bear upon the problems of the hour. His power
as a moral teacher was in the veracity and bold-
ness with which he could utter "Thus saith the
Lord." He had no new message of his own. He
did not even restate the enduring verities in different terms. He never attempted, like Wordsworth, a fresh philosophical grasp upon the

frame of things. Like most of the prophets and
saints, he took the accepted moralities, the familiar religious formulas of his day, and through
his own fervor breathed into them life and passion. But he creates no novel world for the spirit
of man; he opens no undreamed horizons to the
imagination.

We must fall back upon Whittier's gift of
fiery and tender speech. It is the case, after
all, of a Marino Faliero, of an old man elo-
quent. And this is precisely what one would
like to know : does Whittier to-day, fifty years
after the full maturing of his powers, and fifteen
years after his death, either compel or persuade
his countrymen to listen to him?

It is easier to ask this question than to answer it. Our people as a whole respond quickly
to personal leadership. They have an immense
latent capacity for moral and political enthusiasm. But there is no master voice in the
world of letters to which the American people
are now listening. In Whittier's early man-
hood he set himself deliberately to learn the
principles of true liberty from the prose of
Milton and of Burke. There are few greater

names in our literature than these. But aside from the perfunctory reading of extracts for school and college examinations, who is reading Milton and Burke to-day? Who is reading Byron and Shelley, poets of emancipation, kin to Whittier by many bonds of sympathy, and far transcending him in poetic variety, power, and beauty? The mind of the American people is occupied with other concerns. For that matter, there is not a single living poet, in any country of the globe, who is generally recognized as a commanding voice. Tennyson was the last. That others will arise in due time no one who knows the history of humanity can doubt. But they have not yet come.

Meantime our own people, at least, no longer look to the poets—as they certainly did in other days—for inspiration and guidance in the performance of public duty. Whittier's "Massachusetts to Virginia," Lowell's "The Present Crisis," Mrs. Howe's "Battle Hymn of the Republic," unquestionably did influence the emotions and the will of millions of Americans. That any political verse would to-day affect our public policy is very doubtful. A single illustration may serve. In 1900, when the question of forcible retention of the Philippines was still a debated one, and considerations of national duty, self-interest, and pride were struggling together in the public mind, Mr. William Vaughn Moody published his "Ode in Time of Hesitation." Many critics of poetry hailed it as the finest political poem produced in this country since Lowell's "Commemoration Ode." Yet noble in thought and masterly in execution though it was, it may be doubted whether Mr. Moody's poem affected the mind of the nation in the slightest degree; and it would be interesting to know whether one spectator in a thousand of Mr. Moody's play, "The Great Divide," has ever even heard of the "Ode in Time of Hesitation."

But the mere fact that political poets are quoted below par to-day — if they may fairly be said to be quoted at all — does not prove that the public is justified in its indifference, or that the poets are in the wrong. On the contrary, it happens that upon at least two of the issues immediately before the American people Whittier's verse takes radical and uncompromising ground, and that upon both of these issues one may safely venture the assertion that Whittier is absolutely and everlastingly right.

The race-question is the first. Not, of course, the old issue of Slavery. Not the wisdom or unwisdom of that hasty Reconstruction legislation, in which partisan advantage was inextricably confused with the ideal interest of former slaves. The race-question transcends any academic inquiry as to what ought to have been done in 1866. It affects the North as well as the South, it touches the daily life of all of our citizens, individually, politically, humanly. It moulds the child's conception of democracy. It tests the faith of the adult. It is by no means an American problem only. The relation of the white with the yellow and black races is an urgent question all around the globe. The present unrest in India, the wars in Africa, the struggle between Japan and Russia, the national reconstruction of China, the sensitiveness of both Canadian and Californian to Oriental immigration, are impressive signs that the adjustment of race-differences is the greatest humanitarian task now confronting the world. What is going on in our States, North and South, is only a local phase of a world problem.

Now, Whittier's opinions upon that world-problem are unmistakable. He believed, quite literally, that all men are brothers ; that oppression of one man or one race degrades the whole human family ; and that there should be the fullest equality of opportunity. That a mere difference in color should close the door of civil, industrial, and political hope upon any individual was a hateful thing to the Quaker poet. The whole body of his verse is a protest against the assertion of race pride, against the emphasis upon racial differences. To Whittier there was no such thing as a "white man's civilization." The only distinction was between civilization and barbarism. He had faith in education, in equality before the law, in freedom of opportunity, and in the ultimate triumph of brotherhood.

> They are rising, —
> All are rising,
> The black and white together !

This faith is at once too sentimental and too dogmatic to suit those persons who have exalted economic efficiency into a fetish and who have talked loudly at times — though rather less loudly since the Russo-Japanese war — about

the white man's task of governing the back-
ward races. But whatever progress has been
made by the American negro, since the Civil
War, in self-respect, in moral and intellectual
development, and — for that matter — in economic efficiency, has been due to fidelity to
those principles which Whittier and other like-
minded men and women long ago enunciated.
The immense tasks which still remain, alike for
" higher" and for "lower" races, can be worked
out by following Whittier's programme, if they
can be worked out at all.

The second of the immediate issues upon
which Whittier's voice is clear is that of international peace. Though the burdens of mili-
tarism were far less apparent in the middle of
the last century than they are to-day, and the
necessity of allaying race-conflicts by peaceful
means was less instant than now, Whittier belonged to the little band of agitators for peace.
He did not make war against war so vocifer-
ously and tactlessly as some of his later breth-
ren in the same cause. But he faced the
question with perfect clearness of conviction.
The good people who were dissatisfied with
the meagre results of the Hague Conference

of 1907 had better read Whittier's lines on
" The Peace Convention at Brussels " (1848).
Then, as now, there were faithless critics —

With sneering lip, and wise world-knowing eyes —

to point out the folly of this dream of disarmament; the impossibility of persuading the
nations to leave the bloody

Sport of Presidents and Kings

in order

To meet alternate on the Seine and Thames
For tea and gossip, like old country dames.

According to these critics, as Whittier represents them, the delegates to the Convention of
1848, such as Cobden and Sturge and Elihu
Burritt, are merely "cravens" who "plead
the weakling's cant." But Kaisers cannot be
checked by resolutions; guns cannot be spiked
with texts of Scripture; " Might alone is
Right."

So, at least, assert the skeptics, whose case
is put by Whittier, much as Lincoln used to
put the case for his opponents at the bar, much
more skillfully than they could do it for themselves. And thereupon, taking refuge in that
hinterland of religious mysticism whither his

spirit was wont to escape when hard pressed, Whittier foretells, in assured vision, the day when there shall yet be peace on earth. Ultimate international good-will is to him

> The great hope resting on the truth of God.

But it rests, and does not waver.

Time has already done much to justify his faith. To compare the conditions under which the Convention of Brussels met in 1848 with the widely organized efforts, and the very tangible progress, which the workers for international peace have made since 1899, is to become aware how much the sentiment of the civilized world has changed upon this subject. The "faithful few" who journeyed to Brussels at their own charges and upon their own initiative have become the duly accredited representatives of forty-four powers, covering the territory of the globe. The Hague Conference was the first real world-assembly, and its work was necessarily confused and hampered. But these professional diplomatists, warriors, and lawyers who met at The Hague are not in advance of, and many of them are far behind, the sentiment of the common people of their respective countries. The popular dissatisfaction with the concrete results of the Conference is the best proof of the progress of the cause with which Whittier was identified.

After all, then, and in spite of every limitation, Whittier's verse does penetrate to the essential concerns of humanity. If Goethe's famous lines are true, and only those who have eaten their bread in tears have learned to know the heavenly powers, then Whittier was an initiate. He knew what it meant to toil, to renounce, to cherish unfulfilled but indefeasible dreams. That note of tenderness which Longfellow found and loved in mediæval literature was native to the author of "The Pennsylvania Pilgrim." Save for their lack of creed and formula, Whittier's hymns might have been composed in the thirteenth century, so utterly simple is their faith. He believed that "altar, church, priest and ritual will pass away"; yet his hymns, like those of many another former heretic and iconoclast, are sung to-day in all the churches. Mr. Pickard notes that in a collection of sixty-six hymns made for the use of the World's Parliament of Religions in 1893, nine were from Whittier, a larger number than from any other poet. In his early editorials he made effective use of the current conventional religious vocabulary, but for his hymns he chose the simple language of the followers of the Inner Light, unfreighted with the old burdens of dogmatism. Here again Time has been on the poet's side, and Whittier's verse has coöperated with the very general tendency to cast off dogmatic trammels and the worn conventionalities of religious expression. It would not be strange if his ultimate influence were to be that of a mystic. Controversy made him a poet, and his pictures of hearth and home and country-side confirmed his fame; his human sympathy still brings his verse into touch with vital political and social issues; but his abiding claim upon the remembrance of his countrymen may yet be found to lie in the wistful tenderness, the childlike simplicity, with which he turned to the other world.

THE EDITOR WHO WAS
NEVER THE EDITOR

The Editor who was never the Editor

Upon the wall of the Atlantic office, among the portraits of former editors, there may be seen a fine open face, with striking eyes and a beard worn longer than is now the fashion. It is a fair likeness of Francis H. Underwood, the projector of the magazine. At least four years before the Atlantic came into being, he originated the plan, engaged the contributors, and but for the failure of a publisher would have enjoyed the full credit of the enterprise. When the magazine was finally launched, in 1857, Underwood was still the initiating spirit. It was he who pleaded with the reluctant head of the firm of Phillips, Sampson & Co. As "our literary man," in Mr. Phillips's comfortable proprietary phrase, he sat at the foot of the table among the guests at that well-known dinner where the project of the

[205]

magazine was first made public. He visited England to secure the services of the first British contributors. Recognizing that Lowell's name was of the highest importance to the success of the new venture, Underwood loyally accepted the position of "office editor," as assistant to his more gifted friend. When the breaking up of the firm of Phillips, Sampson & Co., in 1859, threw the ownership of the magazine into the hands of Ticknor and Fields, Underwood went out of office, as did Lowell in due time. He had thereafter a varied and honorable, although a somewhat disappointed career, which has already been sketched in the Atlantic [1] by the sympathetic pen of J. T. Trowbridge.

A graceful writer, and a warm-hearted, enthusiastic associate of men more brilliant than himself, Underwood's name is already shadowed by that forgetfulness which awaits the second-rate men of a generation rich in creative energy. For it must be admitted that his ability was not of the first order; as the slang of the athlete has it, he never quite "made the team." But he played the literary game devotedly, honestly,

[1] "The Author of *Quabbin*," January, 1895.

and always against better men ; he became, in
short, a model of the "scrub" player. The
scrubs, as every one knows, get a good dinner
at the end of the season, listen to the thanks
of the coaches, and then are straightway forgotten.

Underwood, however, gave alms to oblivion
by several useful volumes, and by keeping an
extraordinary scrap-book.[1] In two huge leather-
backed volumes are pasted hundreds upon hundreds of letters received during his forty years
of correspondence with many of the foremost
American and English writing men. There are
a dozen or more from Lowell, many from
Emerson, nearly forty from Holmes, and about
fifty from Whittier. The letters are arranged
alphabetically, and run from Alcott and Allibone
to Robert C. Winthrop and Elizur Wright; and
in point of time they range from Richard H.
Dana the elder, who helped found "The North
American Review" in 1815, down to authors
who are still struggling. Many of these letters
throw light upon the unwritten history of the
Atlantic, besides illustrating the literary con-

[1] Kindly loaned to me by its present owner, George F.
Babbitt of Boston.

ditions which prevailed in this country during Underwood's life. One of the earliest letters, for example, is from N. P. Willis, then a name of first rank in the literary profession. Underwood, who was born in Enfield, Massachusetts, in 1825, had left Amherst College without graduating, had gone to Kentucky, taught school, studied law, and married. But he yearned for a literary career, and sent specimens of his poetry to Mr. Willis, who was then in Washington. The veteran's reply is interesting, and his bland phrase, "Your poetry is as good as Byron's was at the same stage of progress," betrays both a kind heart and a long editorial experience.

WASHINGTON, *April* 29 [*about* 1848].

MY DEAR SIR,—Your letter forwarded to me here is just received, and I hasten to comply with your request, tho' young poets ask advice very much as lovers do after they are *irrevocably engaged.* In the first place, however, I should always advise *against* adopting the literary profession, for at the best, it is like making waggon-traces of your hair — wholly insufficient for wants which increase as the power gives way. Your poetry is as good as Byron's was at the same stage of progress—correct, and evidently inspired, and capable of expansion into stuff for fame. But there are many men of the same calibre who would go on, and starve up to the empty honor of being remembered (first) when dead, were it not that they could turn their more common powers to account, and live by meaner industry. Poetry is an angel in your breast, and you had better not turn her out to be your maid-of-all-work. As to writing for magazines, that is very nearly done with as a matter of profit. The competition for *notoriety alone* gives the editors more than they can use. You could not *sell* a piece of poetry now in America. The literary avenues are all overcrowded, and you cannot live by the pen except as a drudge to a newspaper. Notwithstanding all this, you will probably try it, and all I can say is, — that you shall have my sympathy and what aid I can give you. If you should come to New York and will call on me, I shall be happy to say more than I have time to write.   Yours very truly,

N. P. WILLIS.

Underwood's sojourn in Kentucky increased his native hatred of slavery, and upon his return

to Massachusetts in 1850 he enlisted in the
Free-Soil movement. In 1852 he was appointed
Clerk of the State Senate, Henry Wilson being
its President. His acquaintance with public
men grew rapidly, and by 1853, when he was
but twenty-eight, he conceived the notion of
a new magazine. Some such project had long
been in the air, as is evident from the letters of
Emerson, Alcott, and Lowell, but Underwood
was the first to crystallize it. It was to be anti-
slavery in politics, but was to draw for general
contributions upon the best writers of the country. He succeeded in interesting J. P. Jewett,
who had undertaken the publication of "Uncle
Tom's Cabin" after the over-cautious Phillips
had rejected it, and who was also the publisher
of Whittier's poems. With characteristic eager-
ness Underwood then wrote to desirable contributors, sketching the proposed magazine,
and soliciting their coöperation. In selecting
some of the letters received in reply, the anti-
slavery men shall be heard first. Wendell Phillips was dubious : —

LYNN, *Aug.* 4th [1853].

DEAR FRIEND,— I have given your idea the
best consideration in my power, and am obliged

to come to a different conclusion from Messrs. May and Garrison. I believe the plan has been tried thrice within my time (I mean my anti-slavery life) and has each time failed. I cannot think, therefore, there is much chance for the periodical sketched in your excellent letter. At the same time I am aware my judgment on such a point is worth little; and that an experiment so useful to the general cause of Reform may not be lost, if practicable, I have enclosed your let-ter, with a few lines, to Theodore Parker, asking him to communicate to you his mature opinion on the subject.

Believe me very truly yours,
WENDELL PHILLIPS.
Mr. F. H. UNDERWOOD.

Theodore Parker was no more encourag-ing:—

BOSTON, 11 *Oct.*, 1853.

MY DEAR SIR, — The more I think of your enterprise the less likely it seems to me to suc-ceed at present. You know how the " Com-monwealth " struggled along, paying nothing and hardly enabling Mr. Wright to live. I fear this undertaking would meet with the same fate

[211]

—at first. Of its ultimate triumph I have little doubt. I laid the matter before the gentlemen I spoke of Sunday night, and that seemed to be their opinion.

Mr. Phillips and Dr. Howe know much more about such things than I do, and their opinion would be better than mine. I am sorry to seem to pour cold water on your scheme, for I should be glad to see it succeed — and to help it forward if possible.

Yours faithfully,

THEO. PARKER.

Mr. UNDERWOOD.

John G. Palfrey thought better of the idea, although in the first of the two letters to be quoted, he speaks of the new periodical as "a weekly newspaper." The second letter shows a clearer understanding of the project.

CAMBRIDGE, *Oct.* 10, 1853.

MY DEAR SIR, — I have with great pleasure heard from you of your project of a weekly newspaper, to be devoted to the exposition and defence of anti-slavery principles. I believe that there is an opening for a paper of this description, and I have full confidence in your ability, and that of your proposed coadjutor, to conduct it to the acceptance and advantage of the public.

 With great regard, I am,
   Dear Sir, your friend and servant,
     JOHN G. PALFREY.

      CAMBRIDGE, *Nov.* 22, 1853.

MY DEAR SIR,—I am much gratified to hear that there is a prospect of a speedy accomplishment of your plan of a literary and anti-slavery Monthly Magazine. I shall be very happy to contribute to the work whenever it is in my power. I have little hope, however, of doing so this winter, my time being pretty strictly appropriated till next May.

 With great regard, I am,
   Dear Sir, your friend and servant,
     JOHN G. PALFREY.

James Freeman Clarke was also optimistic:—

      BOSTON, *November* 23, 1853.

MY DEAR SIR, — I received yesterday your favor of the 21st, in reference to the new Magazine about to be published by J. P. Jewett & Co. The plan appears to me an excellent one, and I am especially glad that it is to be started by Publishers whose business energy will place the publication part on such a basis as will, I trust, ensure success to the enterprise.

I shall be happy to be one of the Contributors to such a Magazine, and to write both for the Reformatory and Miscellaneous Departments. . . .

JAMES FREEMAN CLARKE.

F. H. UNDERWOOD, Esq.

The next three letters will serve to illustrate the attitude of the New York writing men.

"Tribune" Office,
NEW YORK, *Nov.* 20, 1853.

DEAR SIR, — Your favor of the 18th is received. It will not be in my power to furnish an article for the first number of your proposed periodical, as I have a number of extra engagements now on hand. If it suits your purpose to receive a monthly letter from New York, giving an off-hand summary of the literature, art, and social gossip of New York, I might incline to furnish it. I will communicate your note to Dana and Fry, and am truly yours,

GEORGE RIPLEY.

F. H. UNDERWOOD, Esq.

The Editor who was never Editor

My dear Sir, — Although I have had so much experience in the starting of new periodicals as to be now habitually doubtful of the success of any, I am still pleased with your project, because I think the country wants an out-and-out independent and freespoken organ of the kind you propose. "Putnam's" is capital in its way, but is necessarily limited in its range of topics. I cannot however promise to write you anything at present, as my engagements are so many and exacting. Nor have I anything on hand, except a few light travelling sketches which would not perhaps suit your purposes.

Mr. Bryant desires me to say that he is already engaged to write for certain periodicals only, and regrets his inability to lend you his name. Mr. Bigelow is not in the city.

With many wishes for your success I have the honour to be

Your obt. Servant,

Parke Godwin.

Canandaigua, N. Y., *Nov.* 24th, '53.

My dear Sir, — Your favor of the 19th, which was sent after me from home, has just reached me. It would give me great pleasure to accede to your request, but it is impossible. My engagements and occupations are such that I could not possibly assist in your enterprise, and while I am honored by your application, and should be flattered by the announcement of my name as a contributor, it would be a promise which I could not perform.

I am compelled to decline, but assure you that I attach the *weightiest* significance to the refractory sentence of your letter, and am

Very truly yours,
GEORGE WILLIAM CURTIS.

Mr. UNDERWOOD.

For the model of an exact, business-like reply, however, demanding the "rate per page (*describing the page*)," we must turn to one of the Concord dreamers.

CONCORD, *Nov.* 22d, '53.

DEAR SIR, — If you will inform me in season at what rate per page (describing the page) you will pay for accepted articles, — returning rejected within a reasonable time, — and your terms are satisfactory, I will forward something

[216]

for your magazine before Dec. 5th, and you shall be at liberty to put my name on the list of contributors.

Yours,

HENRY D. THOREAU.

Apparently Underwood's rejoinder was satisfactory, for Thoreau's next letter was accompanied by an actual manuscript.

CONCORD, *Dec.* 2d, 1853.

DEAR SIR, — I send you herewith a complete article of fifty-seven pages. " Putnam's Magazine" pays me four dollars a page, but I will not expect to receive more for this than you pay to anyone else. Of course you will not make any alterations or omissions without consulting me.

Yours,

HENRY D. THOREAU.

The plan was to issue the first number early in January, 1854, and the contributors, as Thoreau's first letter indicates, were asked to send copy by December 5.

Thomas Wentworth Higginson, then a young minister in Worcester, has printed in his

"Old Cambridge" the letters which he received from Underwood. The first one ran: —

BOSTON, *November* 21, 1853.

DEAR SIR, — Messrs. J. P. Jewett & Co. of this city propose to establish a Literary and Anti-Slavery magazine — commencing probably in January. The publishers have energy and capital, and will spare no pains to make the enterprise completely successful. They will endeavor to obtain contributions from the best writers, and will pay liberally for all they make use of. Politics and the "Humanities," though, of course, prominent as giving character to the Magazine, will occupy but a small portion of its pages. Current literary topics, new books, the Fine Arts, and other matters of interest to the reading public will receive the most careful attention.

I am desired to request you to become a contributor. If you are disposed to favor the project, and have anything written at this time, please forward the MS. with your reply.

If not, please state whether we may expect to receive an article soon — if before December 5th it will materially oblige us. If permitted, we shall announce you as a contributor, in the prospectus. The articles will all be anonymous, as in " Putnam's Monthly."

Your early attention is respectfully solicited. With high regard,

Truly yours,

Francis H. Underwood.

The scrap-book preserves Higginson's reply, — a letter characterized by the prompt helpfulness which the successive editors of the Atlantic have happily experienced for more than half a century.

Worcester, *Nov.* 21, 1853.

Dear Sir, — I hear with great interest of the proposed magazine, though I have grown distrustful of such enterprises, especially when of Boston origin. The publishers you name are in a position to do it, if any are. I gladly contribute my name to the list of writers — and any counsel I can ever give, when needed.

As to the positive amount of literary aid to be expected from me, I must speak very cautiously. I am very much absorbed by necessary writing, speaking and studies, and it is hard to do collateral work ; I have been engaged some

[219]

four months to write an article for the "Christian Examiner" on Collier's Shakespeare; have all the books collected and yet have done about nothing and finally given up that undertaking.

Besides, I have access to "Putnam" for anything of a literary character in prose and verse, — a better paymaster, I suspect, than the new magazine can be expected to be. To be sure, "Putnam" is not . . . reformatory, and I should feel much more interest in yours. But then again I suspect Mr. Jewett would be much more keen on the scent of any theological heresy, however latent, than the editors of " Putnam."

But I know I shall have something *in time* to offer, tho' I have nothing now at hand — nor can I before Dec. 5. I hv. in mind especially an essay wh. will actually give a *new* aspect of the slavery subject! — called " The Romance of Slavery or American Feudalism," grouping the points of analogy between Mediæval slavery and southern. Of Hebrew and Roman slavery there has been an excess of discussion :— of Mediæval serfdom hardly anything is known and yet the analogy is more picturesque and more thorough. I read a lecture on this subject at Salem this winter, but it will not be in condition to print, for a month or two. It will be, in that time, unless I decide to keep it for a lecture.

However it is a new matter to me (your magazine) and these are only first impressions. I answer thus promptly, partly to express my good will and give my name, and partly to suggest some other names, as follows: Rev. D. A. Wasson of Groveland, minister of an Independent Church — a man of rare and growing intellect — author of several verses and a remarkable article on Lord Bacon in the "New Englander."

Miss Anne Whitney of Watertown, Mass., author of two remarkable poems in my "Thalatta"; I know of no American woman with so much poetical genius, now that Mrs. J. R. Lowell is gone.

Miss Eliza Sproat of Philadelphia, author of the original and admirable "Stories for Children and Poets" in the "National Era."

But especially and above all, *William Henry Hurlbut* of Cambridge, Mass., author of those brilliant letters fr. Cuba in "National Era" and of some fine articles (a few years ago) in " N.

such pages as "Putnam's," though it is probable that we shall use a trifle larger type than our New York contemporary. Poetry, of course, we pay for according to value. There are not above six men in America (known to me) to whom I would pay *anything* for poetry. There is no medium; it is good or it is good-for-nothing. Lowell I esteem most; after him Whittier (the last I confidently expect to secure).

The first no. will probably be late — as late as Jan. 5, or even 10th. It is unavoidable. But in Feb. we shall get before the wind.

Mr. Jewett will be liberal as to heresy. Indeed he is almost a heretic himself. For myself I am a member of Mr. Parker's society; but as we must get support moral and pecuniary from the whole community we shall *strive* to offend neither side. In haste,

Most gratefully yours,

FRANCIS H. UNDERWOOD.

Whittier, who was on cordial terms with his publisher, Jewett, writes with enthusiasm: —

AMESBURY, 25, 11 *Mo.*, 1853.

DEAR FRIEND, — I am delighted with the prospect of a *free* magazine. It will go: the

[224]

THE EDITOR WHO WAS NEVER EDITOR

AMESBURY, 6th 12 *Mo.*, 1853.

DEAR SIR,—I regret the failure of the magazine project. I was quite sure of its success.

I sent thee a poem, care of J. P. J. & Co.,
which I will thank thee to return to me immediately, and thereby greatly oblige

Thine truly,

JOHN G. WHITTIER.

Whatever publicity may have been given to
the failure of Underwood's scheme, Longfellow
apparently knew nothing of what had happened,
as the date of the following dilatory note will
show:—

CAMBRIDGE, *February* 17, 1854.

DEAR SIR,—I hope you will pardon me for
having left so long unanswered your letter about
a New Magazine or Literary Paper. The fact is,
I could not say "Yes," and did not want to say
"No"; and therefore said nothing.

Between the two forms proposed, a Magazine, monthly, and a weekly newspaper, I should
have no hesitation in deciding. I very much prefer the latter. You can fire much faster and do
more execution.

As to being a contributor to either, it would

[229]

not at present be in my power. I have already
more engagements on hand than I can conven-
iently attend to, and should feel any addition a
burden and a vexation.

I remain, with best wishes for your success,

Very truly yours,

HENRY W. LONGFELLOW.

By the time Longfellow's letter was written,
however, Underwood had entered the counting-
room of Phillips, Sampson & Co. Here he lost
no opportunities of cultivating the acquaintance
of literary men, and in the course of the next two
or three years he became prominent in the social
gatherings of the Cambridge and Boston writers.
He was one of the leaders of that loosely organized group of diners who after 1857 used to
meet under the name of the "Atlantic" or the
"Magazine" Club, — a gathering often confused with the Saturday Club, although Longfellow's Journal and many other contemporary
writings clearly make the distinction.

The following letter from Professor Felton
gives an agreeable picture of the cordial relations
of the men who were so soon to become contributors to the long-deferred magazine.

[230]

THE EDITOR WHO WAS NEVER EDITOR

CAMBRIDGE, *Friday, Feb* 13, 1856.
in bed

MY DEAR MR. UNDERWOOD, — I am much obliged to you for taking the trouble of informing me of to-morrow's dinner — but it is like holding a Tantalus' cup to my lips. I returned ill ten days ago from Washington, having taken the epidemic that is raging there at the present moment, and have been bed-ridden ever since, living on a pleasant variety of porridge and paregoric. Yesterday I was allowed to nibble a small mutton-chop, but it proved too much for me and — here I am, worse than ever. I have no definite prospect of dining at Parker's within the present century. My porridge is to be reduced to gruel and paregoric increased to laudanum. I am likely to be brought to the condition of the student in Canning's play, —

> " Here doomed to starve on water gru-
> el never shall I see the U-
> niversity of Göttingen,"

and never dine at Parker's again! I hope you will have a jovial time; may the mutton be tender and the goose not tough: May the Moet sparkle like Holmes's wit: May the carving knives be as sharp as Whipple's criticism: May

[231]

the fruits be as rich as Emerson's philosophy:
May good digestion wait on appetite and Health
on both — and I pray you think of me as the
glass goes round. . . .

 Horizontally but ever cordially
    Your friend,
      C. C. FELTON.

 The following note of regret from Emerson
refers to another Saturday dinner arranged by
Underwood.

     CONCORD, 26 *August*, 1856.

MY DEAR SIR, — I did not receive your note
until the Boston train had already gone on Saturday. I am well contented that the Club should
be solidly organized, and grow. I am so irregu-
larly in town, that I dare not promise myself as a
constant member, yet I live so much alone that
I set a high value on my social privileges, and I
wish by all means to retain the right of an occasional seat.

 So, with thanks, and best wishes,
    Yours,
      R. W. EMERSON.

Mr. UNDERWOOD.

Underwood now thought that the time was ripe for bringing the magazine project to the front once more. Mr. Phillips was slow to take an interest in it, but finally agreed to consult Mrs. Harriet Beecher Stowe. He had published her "Dred" in 1856, although he had previously rejected "Uncle Tom's Cabin" through fear of alienating his Southern trade. Mrs. Stowe was instantly enthusiastic over the proposed magazine, and promised her support. It was this fact, as Underwood often said in later years, which decided the wavering mind of the publisher. Then came the famous dinner given by Mr. Phillips on May 5, 1857, to the men whose coöperation was thought to be essential. Although Mr. Arthur Gilman's article, printed in the Atlantic for November, 1907, describes this dinner, it may be interesting to quote Mr. Phillips's own letter about it, as given in Dr. Hale's "James Russell Lowell and his Friends" (p. 157).

[*May* 19, 1857.]

" I must tell you about a little dinner-party I gave about two weeks ago. It would be proper, perhaps, to state that the origin of it was a desire to confer with my literary friends on a somewhat extensive literary project, the particulars of which I shall reserve until you come. But to the party: My invitations included only R. W. Emerson, H. W. Longfellow, J. R. Lowell, Mr. Motley (the 'Dutch Republic' man), O. W. Holmes, Mr. Cabot, and Mr. Underwood, our literary man. Imagine your uncle as the head of such a table, with such guests. The above named were the only ones invited, and they were all present. We sat down at three p. m., and rose at eight. The time occupied was longer by about four hours and thirty minutes than I am in the habit of consuming in that kind of occupation, but it was the richest time intellectually by all odds that I have ever had. Leaving myself and 'literary man' out of the group, I think you will agree with me that it would be difficult to duplicate that number of such conceded scholarship in the whole country besides.

"Mr. Emerson took the first post of honor at my right, and Mr. Longfellow the second at my left. The exact arrangement of the table was as follows:—

MR. UNDERWOOD

CABOT   LOWELL
MOTLEY   HOLMES
LONGFELLOW   EMERSON

PHILLIPS

"They seemed so well pleased that they adjourned, and invited me *to meet them* again tomorrow, when I shall meet the same persons, with one other (Whipple, the essayist) added to that brilliant constellation of philosophical, poetical and historical talent. Each one is known alike on both sides of the Atlantic, and is read beyond the limits of the English language. Though all this is known to you, you will pardon me for intruding it upon you. But still I have the vanity to believe that you will think them the most natural thoughts in the world to me. Though I say it that should not, it was the proudest day of my life."

"In this letter," continues Dr. Hale, "he does not tell of his own little speech, made at the launch. But at the time we all knew of it. He announced the plan of the magazine by saying, 'Mr. Cabot is much wiser than I am. Dr. Holmes can write funnier verses than I can. Mr. Motley

[235]

can write history better than I. Mr. Emerson is a philosopher, and I am not. Mr. Lowell knows more of the old poets than I.' But after this confession he said, 'But none of you knows the American people as well as I do.'"

Exactly what Underwood thought, as he listened to this self-satisfied speech of his employer, is not recorded in his scrap-book. Nor do the letters of the next few weeks throw any light upon the now familiar story of Lowell's accepting the editorship of the new magazine upon the condition that Holmes should become a contributor, and of Holmes's suggestion that it should be christened "The Atlantic Monthly." Who chose John Winthrop's head as a design for the brown cover does not appear.

Underwood, meanwhile, had sailed for England in June to secure contributors. He enjoyed his mission, and his scrap-book contains many hospitable notes from Charles Reade, Wilkie Collins, John Forster, A. H. Clough, and other English writers. Reade was anxious to become acquainted with "any honest publisher who can be brought to see that I am worth one third as much as Thackeray, or

more. . . . 'White Lies' is my best story."
In reply to Underwood's promise that the
Atlantic's rate of payment would be equal to
that offered by the English reviews, James
Hannay replies : —

"With regard to the remuneration, as you
intimated that it was to be regulated by the
best pay here, I may mention that that is a
guinea a page, or sixteen guineas a sheet."

Encouraged by promises of contributions,
Underwood sailed for home, leaving the manuscripts to follow. Some of them, as Mr. Norton
has related (Atlantic for November, 1907), disappeared forever with Mr. Norton's unlucky
trunk. A pleasant note from Shirley Brooks,
of the staff of "Punch," refers to the loss of
his manuscript: —

The Garrick Club,
London, *Oct.* 28, '57.

My dear Sir, — I have been away from
London, or your letter would have been an-
swered long ago. I should be ashamed to look
at its date but for this, and you will have been
sure that the delay was caused in some such
manner.

The mishap to which it refers, (your note,

PARK-STREET PAPERS

Office " Saturday Eve. Post,"
PHILADA., *Aug.* 20th, '57.

MY DEAR SIR, — I have been striving very hard to make kosmos out of the chaos of a MS tale I have for some time had on hand — a thing of shreds and patches it is, at present, existing only in stray sheets, scraps and memoranda — but to save my life I cannot get time enough to build this little world of mine, I have to give so much to the affairs of this other world — the "Post" — of which I am in effect, the governor, and all the more so now since the ostensible chief is away, and everything devolves on me. I am secretly chagrined to think that my little star will not be visible this month in the march of your galaxy, for, dropping similes, I wanted very much to have a paper of mine in your first number. However, man proposes and the "Saturday Post" disposes, so I submit, as you will find less disappointment in doing.

I shall still endeavor to give you a story, — for the second number if possible, or if not, for a later number, — but I beg of you to expect nothing of me, for though my promises are words of fate, I am unable to make them now, my time being already engrossed so much as to make it difficult even to attend to my casual correspondence. And then, besides, when you do get a MS of mine, it is quite likely you will not like it, the revolution and the radicalisms running so naturally to my pen, and my tales being my only present means of securing to myself the luxury of my individual views and opinions.

With many regrets and hopes, and with twice as many good wishes for the prosperity of the coming magazine, I remain very

Truly yours,
WM. D. O'CONNOR.
F. H. UNDERWOOD, Esq.

J. T. Trowbridge's note, accompanying his contribution to the first number, shows that he thought that the name of the magazine was not yet determined upon: —

OGDEN, *Aug.* 24, 1857.

MY DEAR U——, I send you a sketch. I don't know whether it is good or bad. It is a subject I have long wished to write upon ; and on the rec't of your letter, I dashed off the history of John Henry Pendlam. I can swear

[241]

considered by one of my critical friends the best thing I have ever written. I cannot judge of these things myself.

We have been long in reaching the actual first number of the Atlantic. The financial stress of 1857 harassed Messrs. Phillips, Sampson & Co., and publication was nearly suspended, after all. But in October the first issue appeared, under date of November. Underwood's scrapbook contains this highly interesting note from Emerson, concerning editorial suggestions upon two of the four poems which he contributed, in addition to the prose essay on "Illusions," to the initial number. If Lowell suggested, as he apparently did, the substitution of

"If, on the heath, *beneath the moon*,"

for

"If, on the heath, under the moon,"

in the fourth stanza of the "Rommany Girl," he certainly proposed "a new cacophony" where there was undoubtedly an "old one." Emerson changed the line in later years to

"If, on the heath, below the moon."

But it is clear from this note that we owe the

present form of the superb opening line of
" Days," —

> " Daughters of Time, the hypocritic Days,"

to the editor, who had objected to "hypocritical."

CONCORD, Sept. 24, 1857.

DEAR SIR, — I return the proof in which I
have no correction to make. Mr. Lowell showed
a bad rhythm, but I do not quite like the new
word he offered me —

> " beneath the moon,"

where the new cacophony troubles my ears as
much as the old one; and for the second suggestion about the word "hypocritical," he is
right again, but I cannot mend it to-day. If he
will alter them, as he proposed before, or other-
wise, he has my thankful consent.

Yours,
R. W. EMERSON.

Mr. UNDERWOOD.

It is well known, also, that Lowell suggested
to Whittier the peculiar form of the refrain which
adds so greatly to the effectiveness of "Skipper Ireson's Ride." In Lowell's "Letters" we
read : —

[245]

PARK-STREET PAPERS

CAMBRIDGE, *November* 4, 1857.

MY DEAR WHITTIER, — I thank you heartily for the ballad, which will go into the next number. I like it all the better for its provincialism — in all fine pears, you know, we can taste the old *pucker*.

I knew the story well. I am familiar with Marblehead and its dialect, and as the burthen is intentionally provincial, I have taken the liberty to print it in such a way as shall give the peculiar accent — thus —

> " Cap'n Ireson for his horrd hort
> Was torred and feathered and corried in a corrt."

That's the way I 've always "horrd it" — only it began "Old Flud Ireson." What a good name Ireson (son of wrath) is for the hero of such a history. . . .

The scrap-book contains Whittier's reply: —

AMESBURY, 6th, 11th *Mo.*, 1857.

DR· FRIEND, — I thank thee for sending the proof of Cap Ireson, with thy suggestions. I adopt them, as thou wilt see, mainly. It is an improvement. As it stands now, I like the thing well — "hugely," as Capt Shandy would say.

As to the pecuniary allusion of thy note, I

[246]

am sorely in want of money (as who is not at
this time) — but of course will await your convenience.

The magazine *will, shall, must* succeed. The
election of Banks is a good beginning for it.
Thy friend,
John G. Whittier.

That the ballad made an immediate impression is seen in this note from Fitz-James
O'Brien, who writes about the acceptance of
his brilliant story "The Diamond Lens": —

Harper's, Franklin Sq're,
Nov. 28th [1857].

Dear Sirs, — I am much pleased that my
story has met your approval, and shall be glad
at some future time to present you with other
articles.

I have not calculated the number of pages
which the "Diamond Lens" will make, and
will thank you to have the computation made
and remit to me the amount according to whatever scale of prices you see fit to include it in.

It will be in a great measure a labor of love
to write for a magazine of so high a tone as the

[247]

Atlantic. I have long felt the want of a channel in which to place articles on which I might bestow labor and thought. Here in New York we are far too apt to neglect the higher aims.

Will you permit me to express the great pleasure I have experienced in reading "Skipper Ireson's Ride" in your last number. It abounds in lyrical fire, pathos and strength.

Yours truly,
FITZ-JAMES O'BRIEN.

Messrs. PHILLIPS, SAMPSON & Co.

This reminds me that Thomas Bailey Aldrich, writing in 1897 to a member of the Atlantic's staff who had prepared a sketch of the first forty years of the magazine, referred thus to O'Brien's story : —

". . . I am sorry that the Atlantic did not put in its claim to being the father of the short story. Of course there were excellent short stories before the Atlantic was born — Poe's and Hawthorne's — but the magazine gave the short story a place which it had never before reached. It began with 'The Diamond Lens' of Fitz-James O'Brien, and ended with — well, it has not ended yet."

[248]

The praise elicited by the early numbers is fairly represented by this note from Henry Ward Beecher:—

BROOKLYN, *Oct.* 31, '57.

MY DEAR SIR,—The Atlantic has a good look—robust and bold. I hope for it a historic reputation. As New England has been the Brain of America, it would be a pity if her mouth did not speak worthy of her head and heart.

Very truly yours,

H. W. BEECHER.

Although the authorship of the articles was supposed to be kept secret, a privately printed list of the authors in each number was soon sent out to newspaper reviewers and other friends of the magazine. It was not until the tenth volume, however, in 1862, that an index of authors was printed at the completion of each volume. The first signed articles to appear were Harriet Hosmer's "Process of Sculpture" and Goldwin Smith's "England and America," in December, 1864. Occasional signed articles followed, such as William M. Rossetti's in 1866 and George Eliot's in May, 1870, but it was not until July, 1870, that signatures were regularly used. Inasmuch as the names of the more prominent contributors engaged were printed in the initial advertising pages, it was not difficult to guess the authorship of most of the articles. But even without this, discerning readers were at once aware of the high quality of the new periodical. Wilkie Collins wrote from London:—

> 11 Harley Place, Marylebone Road,
> LONDON, *December* 30th, 1857.

MY DEAR SIR,— . . . Pray don't trouble yourself to answer this letter, until my contribution to the magazine reaches you—when I shall be glad to hear of its safe arrival. I shall look out with great interest for the story to which you refer in the third number. Excepting the difficulties of finding good tellers of tales (sorely felt here, let me say, as well as in America), with such men as Longfellow and Emerson to head your list of contributors, I cannot think that you need fear the rivalry of any magazine in any region of the civilized world.

> Believe me to remain
> > Very cordially yours,
> > > WILKIE COLLINS.

F. H. UNDERWOOD, Esq.

THE EDITOR WHO WAS NEVER EDITOR

Charles Reade, several of whose vigorous and pugnacious epistles were preserved by Underwood, wrote in the autumn of 1858:—

6 Bolton Row, Mayfair, Oct. 10.

Dear Sir,—I beg to acknowledge yours of date Sept. 28, and as requested answer by return mail. I will never under any circumstances submit a MS. of mine to the chance of any other writer comprehending it and seeing its merit. If therefore *that* is an absolute condition, you will never see a line of mine in the Atlantic Monthly while I live. The stories you do publish in the Monthly could never have been selected by any judge competent to sit in judgment on me. We had better wait a little. You will find that every word of fiction I produce will succeed *more* or *less;* this in a world crammed with feeble scribblers is a sufficient basis for treaty. As to the exact *manner* of success no man can pronounce on it beforehand.

"White Lies" which you seem to think has failed has on the contrary been a greater success than "It is Never Too Late to Mend." At all events it is so represented to me by the Publishers and this not in complimentary

[251]

phrases only, of which you and I know the value, but in figures that represent cash.

Yet, as you are aware, it had to resist a *panic*. A truce to egotism, and let me congratulate you on the circulation and merit of your monthly. It is a wonderful product at the price. Good paper, excellent type, and the letters disengaged so that one can read it.

Then as for the matter, the stories are no worse than "Blackwood's" and "Frasers'," etc., etc., and some of the other matter is infinitely beyond our monthly and trimestral scribblers, being genuine in thought and English in expression. Whereas what passes for criticism here is too often a mere mixture of Cuck-oo and hee-haw. A set of conventional phrases turned not in English but in Norman French and the jargon of the schools.

After five and twenty years of these rotten old cabbage stalks without a spark of thought, novelty or life among them, I turn my nose to such papers as your "Autocrat of the Breakfast Table," etc. with a sense of relief and freshness. . . . Success attend you, and when you are *ripe for   Yours truly* CHARLES READE

let me know.

Meanwhile Underwood was unweariedly active, not only at his desk but in the pleasures of good fellowship with other musical, artistic, and literary spirits. His scrap-book contains many a charming whimsical letter from F. J. Child, who usually addressed him as " Sottobosco," and was wont to drop into French or Italian for a convenient word. Even the self-contained Emerson writes about the luck which goes to a dinner in anything but a transcendental vein: —

CONCORD, 21 *Nov.* [1857].

DEAR SIR, — I am sorry I cannot come to town to-day, and join your strong party at dinner. I shall be in town on Tuesday, probably, and I will not fail to come to your Counting Room and I will think in the meantime what I can do. From what you say of the club dinner, I have no dream of any such self-denying ordinance as you intimate. There is always a good deal of luck goes to a dinner, and if ours was a heavy one, as you say it was, there is the more reason to believe the luck will turn and be with us next time. But I was in the dark about it, and only regretted that I

[253]

cept it. I am attending a hearing before a Railroad Committee at the State House which is to go on at 3 P. M. and would leave no time for the dinner.

My best wishes attend the Magazine, its editors and contributors. May it never blow up! I think the February number surpassed any promises that were made for it—and that the Doctor's exquisite little "Nautilus" is in rather a finer strain than anything he has given us before.

Very truly yours,

E. R. HOAR.

F. H. UNDERWOOD, Esq.

Meanwhile Charles Eliot Norton was writing from Newport, December 25, 1857: "I am very glad to hear of the success of the Atlantic. The third number certainly shows no falling off. . . . If you care for this that follows from Ruskin you are welcome to have it published. . . . Mr. Ruskin says: 'I was delighted with the magazine and all that was in it. What a glorious thing of Lowell's that is, — but it is too bad to quiz Pallas. I can stand it about anybody but her.'"

A little later Mr. Norton, with a kindness which has not ceased during half a century, was commending a new English story writer to the Atlantic's attention, — no less a personage than "*Mr*. George Eliot"!

NEWPORT, Monday [1858].

DEAR MR. UNDERWOOD, . . . "Adam Bede" seems to me the best novel in points of artistic development of the story and clear drawing of character that we have had for a long time. It does not show so much imagination as Miss Brontë's books, — nor such fine feminine insight and tenderness of feeling as Mrs. Gaskell's.

But if you could get Mr. George Eliot to write a story for the Atlantic I think it would be sure to answer well. It would require a handsome offer to tempt him, — for his book is universally popular in England, and he can make his own terms with the publishers. . . .

Ever truly yours,

CHARLES E. NORTON.

That there were some thorns in the editorial cushions, however, is plainly indicated in some

[257]

ber, Lowell, apparently without consulting Mr.
Godwin, added six pages of his own, expressing
"contempt" and "humiliation" at the administration. The editor's portion of the article was
indeed separated from the contributor's by a
blank line, and the article was of course unsigned. But Godwin was very angry, as his letter to poor Underwood, who had apparently
attempted an explanation, will show: —

NEW YORK, *March* 26, '58.

MY DEAR MR. UNDERWOOD, — The pur-
port of your note, if I understand it, is, that
"your publishers" do not like my articles,
because a certain alleged want of "fervor" dis-
appoints the newsvenders. As this is the first
expression of opinion that I have had from anybody, connected with the magazine, I am glad
to be enlightened.

The deficiency imputed to them, or any other
deficiency, would have been a good reason for
suppressing them, altogether: but it is not a
good reason for mutilating them; nor does it
justify any man in appending to them, without
my knowledge or consent, several pages of his
own remarks.

[260]

These articles were written after a careful survey of the whole field of discussion, — from a pretty good knowledge of the state of public opinion: and in view of the yet nascent tendencies of parties. They were addressed to the reason and good sense of the American people rather than to the feelings and prejudices of factions. I constructed them also — particularly in the omissions — with reference to the near and probable future of Parties, so that the Cause of the Right would not be injured by any needless virulence, — and yet the truth be quite openly and roundly asserted. I did not hope to satisfy the "fervid" Abolition sentiment of New England: nor to write sensation articles for the newsvenders: but I did hope to make the Magazine gradually a power and an authority in the best minds of the country. It seems that I have made a mistake: and that my considerate sentences are unsuited to the "fervid" atmosphere of Boston.

Now, this is a mistake that I cannot, because I will not correct. I have never yet written for mere factions or localities. I have studied the politics of this country many years, with an average degree of intelligence, I hope: with the sin-

[261]

cerity of a patriot, I know: and also in the large and thoughtful spirit of philosophy. I am therefore as a writer, no "thunderer" — as the gentleman who attempts to supply my deficiencies is, — perhaps, — and consequently, as thunder is needed, I willingly resign my place to him. I shall hereafter look with much interest towards the demonstrations of this new Love, — hoping that you too may be satisfied!

I learn from your note that Mr. Lowell was the person who took upon himself to curtail my article, and then to substitute his own matter. For Mr. Lowell's general poetic and literary abilities I have a high respect: but I have never heard of him as a peculiarly competent political thinker or writer: and, however that may be, I must say frankly that I should prefer to put my writings before the public without his "improvements."

Under these circumstances I do not see how you can expect from me the promised article on the "Decadence of Democracy"; a part of what I reserved to say in that Mr. Lowell has anticipated, and the rest, I imagine, would be exposed to the same liabilities the former articles have been. The conditions are not accordant with my sense of self-respect. At the same time, as I may not have contributed my full number of pages according to our original agreement, I will endeavor to satisfy the terms of the contract in some other line.

The sketch entitled "Attilee" you do not refer to, — nor my offer of the history, — and I beg leave therefore to withdraw both from your consideration.

You speak of "conflicting interests and opinions," — but let me say that I have had no conflict with anybody. I was solicited to write, and did so (often in too great hurry under your urgency) : and since what I have written does not suit you, you have a perfect right to say so. I should have liked it better if you had been more direct and frank in your method of communicating the fact; but I certainly acquit you personally of any unkindness or unfriendliness in the premises. My sentiments as to Mr. Lowell's proceedings are another affair.

Fred Cozzens and I had arranged to go and eat a dinner with you on Saturday: but as we are afraid that we should be found very cold and dull clods amid the fervid and glowing wits who surround Maga, our prudence has got the bet-

ter of our valour: we shall instead warm up our
heavy clay with some less Olympian brewages.
                    Yours truly,
                        PARKE GODWIN.

Other editorial embarrassments were of a
slighter character. When Underwood asked
T. B. Aldrich to alter his "Blue Bell" rhymes,
at Lowell's request, the younger poet refused,[1]
and withdrew the verses. The scrap-book reveals the fact that it was Lowell himself who
had desired the alteration, and who was now
wondering what had become of the poem. But
the Atlantic never saw it again; although Aldrich ultimately adopted the editorial suggestion.

                                    [1858.]

MY DEAR UNDERWOOD, — You will remember that I asked you to send the "Blue Bells"
to Mr. Aldrich for an alteration in one of the
stanzas. When that is made it shall go in. I
think you have it.

I am going to make a gaol-delivery of verse
in the next number.
                    Yrs. ever,
                        J. R. L.

[1] Aldrich's note is printed on p. 152.

One is tempted to quote all of Aldrich's inimitable notes to Underwood, as well as letters
from Sainte-Beuve and other foreign writers,
and many a friendly line from Holmes and
Whittier. How characteristic of the Autocrat is
the blithe "let her slide" of the following epistle,
referring to the lines "The Living Temple"
(May, 1858).

MY DEAR MR. UNDERWOOD,—If it is pos-
sible to change a word in my last poem I can
get rid of a repetition I have just noticed. If it
is too late, let her slide.
Instead of
  " But warmed by that mysterious flame "
Read
  " But warmed by that unchanging flame."
      Yours, O. W. H.
Monday evening.

But the end of Underwood's editorial work
upon the magazine was at hand. Mr. Phillips's
death in the summer of 1859, following the
death of Mr. Sampson, led to the suspension
and dissolution of the firm. A letter from a
worried New York poet paints the situation:—

Debenture Room, Custom House,
NEW YORK, *Sept.* 7, '59.

DEAR SIR,—I wrote Messrs. Phillips and
Sampson a business note two or three weeks
ago, asking them to send me a check for a poem
of mine in the August number of the Atlantic
Monthly. No check has reached me; no no-
tice has been taken of the note. As both members of the firm have "gone dead," I suppose
it useless to write them beyond the Styx, so I
trouble you. The *house* lives, I suppose, if the
men die. I want the money for the poem, whatever it may be, or I want to know that I am not
to have it, so that I may forget all about it, and
turn to

"Fresh fields and pastures new."

Will you not see to the affair and oblige me?
Have a check, or the money sent me (my direc-
tion is over leaf) or tell me for what sum to draw
on Phillips and Sampson. At any rate answer
this note, that I may know that it reaches you.
Perhaps I had better tell you that the poem was
printed under the head of "The End of All."

Respectfully, etc.,

R. H. STODDARD.

F. H. UNDERWOOD, Esq.
Boston.

THE EDITOR WHO WAS NEVER EDITOR

A kindly note from George William Curtis,
two weeks later, is like the fall of the curtain : —

NEW YORK, 20 *Sep.*, 1859.

MY DEAR SIR, — Will you send me all the
unused MSS. of Mr. Cranch's that you have,
and can you tell me the probable destiny of the
plates of "Huggermugger" and "Kobbotozo"?
Was the contract for a limited term, — I have
forgotten.

The news of the suspension of your house fell
heavily upon all of us who were interested in
the publishing of good books and of the Atlantic. My constant employments have engaged
me elsewhere, — but could not lead me beyond
the heartiest sympathy with the spirit of the
magazine and admiration of its excellence.

What will you do? Can I keep you here in
New York?

Very truly yours,
GEORGE WILLIAM CURTIS.

The magazine itself was transferred to the
house of Ticknor and Fields, in a fashion amus-
ingly described in the Contributors' Club in November, 1907. Both Lowell and Underwood

[267]

lingered in office for a while, the former until May, 1861. J. L. Motley, writing to Underwood from London on November 11, 1860, in praise of the Atlantic, says, "I am writing this under the impression that you are still editor of the magazine." But the happiest part of Underwood's life was over. He now moved from Cambridge to South Boston. For many years he served as Clerk of the Superior Court, devoting his spare hours to music and literature. His friends remained faithful, and the following polyglot note from Lowell, inviting him to an evening of whist with John Bartlett and John Holmes, is but one of the invitations which testify to the intimacy of such companionship.

ELMWOOD, Thursday.

MY DEAR UNDERWOOD, — Come early and come often. J'ai tout arrangé: les deux Jeans y seront de bonne heure, et nous en ferons une vraie nuit de vacances. Votre billet, tout cordial qu'il était, et plein de bonté à mon regard, m'a vraiment réchauffé le cœur. Vous trouverez un lit chez nous, et retournerez à la Cour Supérieure de bon matin, y portant un mal de tête des meilleurs, si le vieux Bourbon et les heures

tardes n'ont pas perdu de force. Venite, dunque,
a che ora vi piacerà, e sarete il benvenuto!

Affectionately yours,

J. R. L.

In 1871 and 1872 Underwood issued Hand-
books of British and American authors, and the
correspondence involved in these tasks, as well
as in his biographies of Longfellow, Whittier,
and Lowell, is well represented in his scrap-
book. There are long letters, for example, from
Parkman and Motley, setting forth their aims
in the great historical undertakings to which
their lives were so largely devoted.

One passage from a letter of Parkman attempts to explain why Underwood had not
enjoyed a greater prestige. He was "neither
a Harvard man nor a humbug"!

50 Chestnut St., *April* 15, 1875.

MY DEAR MR. UNDERWOOD, — . . . I wish
that your connection with the Atlantic could
have been continued long enough to give your
literary powers and accomplishments a fair
chance of just recognition. It is for the interest
of us all that men like you should be rated

[269]

HOLDERNESS, N. H.,
7th *Mo.* 27, 1885.

MY DEAR UNDERWOOD, — I have been away for some time trying to gain some strength from the hills, and have just seen a paragraph in the papers by which I am glad to learn of thy appointment as U. S. Consul at Glasgow. I am heartily rejoiced at it, and hasten to congratulate thee. President Cleveland has done a handsome thing in thus recognizing one of the "literary fellows" who had the honor of the first editorship of the Atlantic Monthly.

I have been in Boston only once for the last year, and then only for a day or two. I wish I could see thee before thy departure for Glasgow, but that is not possible in my state of health. I must not leave here during this hot weather. I am glad our country and its literature is to be so well represented in the land of Burns and Scott.

God bless thee and prosper thee !
Thy old friend,
JOHN G. WHITTIER.

These later notes from Whittier refer to the biography upon which Underwood was en-

[272]

gaged. They are vigorous, and very characteristic.

AMESBURY, 4 *Mo*. 14, 1883.

DEAR FD., — . . . Don't make too big a
book, and don't try to account for everything
I have written or not written, or done, or not
done. A mere mention of the fact that I have
written in my first attempts a great [deal] of
prose and rhyme which I would not now in-
sult the reader by reproducing, is enough.
And do not forget that I have lived a hard
life outside of my verse making. I am a *man*
and not a mere verse maker. Thine truly,

JOHN G. WHITTIER.

AMESBURY, 6 *Mo*. 14 [1883].

DEAR F. H. UNDERWOOD, — . . . I see one
of the chapters headed " Beginnings of Fame."
I don't think at the time mentioned the word
Fame is applicable. It is safe to say that there
are now in the United States ten thousand boys
and girls who can write better verses than mine
at their age. The single fact is that my first
scribblings are very poor and commonplace.
Thine truly,

JOHN G. WHITTIER.

[273]

Park-Street Papers

Asquam, Holderness, N. H.,
7 *Mo.* 21, 1883.

Dear friend,—I am grateful for thy generous estimate of my writings in " Characteristics," but I fear the critics will not agree with thee. Why not anticipate them, and own up to faults and limitations which everybody sees, and none more clearly than myself. Touch upon my false rhymes and Yankeeisms : confess that I sometimes " crack the voice of melody and break the legs of time." Pitch into " Mogg Megone." That " big Injun" strutting round in Walter Scott's plaid, has no friends and deserves none. Own that I sometimes choose unpoetical themes. Endorse Lowell's " Fable for Critics " that I mistake occasionally simple excitement for inspiration. In this way we can take the wind out of the sails of ill-natured cavillers. I am not one of the master singers and don't pose as one. By the grace of God I am only what I am, and don't wish to pass for more.

I return the sheets, with this note. Think of my suggestions and act upon them if it seems best to thee. Always thy friend,

John G. Whittier.

THE EDITOR WHO WAS NEVER EDITOR

AMESBURY, 1 *Mo.* 20, 1884.

MY DEAR UNDERWOOD, — I am very sorry
to find thee lay so much stress on dragging to
light all the foolish things written by me, and
which I hate the thought of. For mercy's sake
let the dead rest. (1) in regard to " Mogg
Megone " (a poem I wish was in the Red Sea),
— I know Benjamin had it, I thought in New
York. It seems he was Ed. of the " N. E.
Magazine " & published it there. (2) Abolition poem by Isaac Knapp. I know nothing
of it. All my anti-slavery poems are in my
collected works. I see no use in setting all
the literary ghouls to digging for something I
have written in my first attempts at rhyme. I
detest the whole of it. . . .

Ever and truly thy friend,
JOHN G. WHITTIER.

Underwood's experiences in Great Britain,
both at Glasgow and later at Edinburgh, —
where he was Consul during Cleveland's second
administration, — were touched upon in Mr.
Trowbridge's article. Between the two con-
sulships he wrote a novel, " Quabbin," in
which he described from that benign distance

[275]

his native town. He received many social honors during his residence abroad, and the degree of LL.D. was conferred upon him by the University of Glasgow. He made friends, as always and everywhere, and the most brilliant of living English writers is represented in the scrap-book by some letters inquiring into the value of certain American securities, which Underwood had recommended him to purchase. To name these securities now might invoke the Comic Spirit.

Underwood never came home to that world which had more or less grown away from him. He died at Edinburgh in 1894. Versatile in gifts and genial in spirit, he was associated, as we have seen, with some of the best men of his day, but he himself never quite "arrived." There were Celts of old time who "always went forth to the fight, but they always fell." One likes them none the worse for that. During the Civil War, Underwood's fertile brain devised a curious project, which had no other result, apparently, than the creation of one more remarkable autograph for his scrap-book. He wished to start a saw-mill in Florida. Every magazine editor, as is well known, has his mo-

[276]

ments of keen desire to be running a saw-mill
somewhere. But Underwood picked out an
actual spot, then under occupation by Federal
troops, and addressed a respectful letter to
President Lincoln, setting forth the benefits
to the nation which would accrue from the said
saw-mill through the promotion of emigration
to Florida. Here is the very document, thrown
carelessly into the scrap-book, endorsed by
leading citizens of Boston, with Ex-Governor
Boutwell at the head, by Charles Sumner and
Henry Wilson, Senators from Massachusetts,
by Major-General Gillmore, then at Hilton
Head, and by the President of the United
States : —

I fully approve, subject to the discretion
and control of the Commanding General.
March 26, 1864.

A. LINCOLN.

A saw-mill in Florida! What a castle in
Spain, for this editor who was never the Editor!

𝕮𝖍𝖊 𝕽𝖎𝖛𝖊𝖗𝖘𝖎𝖉𝖊 𝕻𝖗𝖊𝖘𝖘

CAMBRIDGE . MASSACHUSETTS

U . S . A